# Windows To My World

# Windows To My World

*A Collection of Poetry
Depicting Real Life For Many*

Deborah Elmore

Copyright © 2014 by Deborah Elmore.

| ISBN: | Softcover | 978-1-4691-7808-0 |
| | eBook | 978-1-4691-7809-7 |

All rights reserved. No part of this book may be reproduced or transmitted in any form or by any means, electronic or mechanical, including photocopying, recording, or by any information storage and retrieval system, without permission in writing from the copyright owner.

Rev. Date: 08/29/2014

Xlibris LLC
1-888-795-4274
www.Xlibris.com
540758

This book is dedicated to my Daughter Desara'e Elmore
She has always been a token of strength and encouragement for me.
Courageous, compassionate, reliable, and determined to win at anything she puts her mind to.
She has grown up to become a beautiful woman, a wonderful mother and an awesome friend who even in childhood was wise beyond her years.

Thank you daughter for being the wind beneath my wings.

I Love You!

### State of Connecticut

By Her Excellency M. Jodi Rell, Governor: an

# Official Statement

*O*n behalf of the State of Connecticut,
I, M. JODI RELL, Governor,
take great pleasure in
congratulating
*Deborah Ann Elmore*
on the occasion of your
graduation from
*Connecticut Office of Faith-Based and Community Initiatives -
Connecticut FaithWorks Community Development
Leadership Institute.*

*A*s a graduate of the Connecticut FaithWorks Community Development Leadership Institute you have acquired the tools to develop plans to increase assets in distressed areas in your communities and reduce the negative impacts of poverty. The skills you have gained through this program have prepared you to play an important role in revitalizing your community, establishing sustainable economic development initiatives, attracting investments, building wealth and encouraging entrepreneurship.

*Y*our commitment and drive to improve the quality of life in your community is an inspiration to all of Connecticut's residents and a testament to your strength and determination. It is an honor to congratulate you and I wish you the very best in all your future endeavors.

*T*herefore, I, M. Jodi Rell, Governor of the State of Connecticut, do hereby officially convey honor and recognition upon
*Deborah Ann Elmore*
in the State of Connecticut.

# CONTENTS

The Journey ............................................................... 13
Born Again ................................................................ 14
Ten Dollars ............................................................... 16
Dressing Up My Pain ....................................................... 18
Jesus Is Gonna Get You .................................................... 20
The Fight ................................................................. 22
The War Zone .............................................................. 24
Coke Addict ............................................................... 26
Who's Running The Circus? ................................................. 28
Different ................................................................. 30
I Found Me ................................................................ 31
Hurt By The Church ........................................................ 32
Holla Back!!! ............................................................. 34
The Truth ................................................................. 36
If People Told The Truth .................................................. 38
The Wilderness ............................................................ 40
Life's Lessons ............................................................ 41
Round Two ................................................................. 43
Canning ................................................................... 45
Invisible ................................................................. 47
Nikka ..................................................................... 49
God Is Calling ............................................................ 51
The White House ........................................................... 53
But God ................................................................... 55
Searching ................................................................. 57
Eighteen With A Bullet .................................................... 59
The Role Model ............................................................ 60
This Is Not My Daughter ................................................... 63
The Big Dogs .............................................................. 65
The Brick ................................................................. 67
Never Came Home ........................................................... 69

| | |
|---|---|
| Where's Our Party? | 72 |
| Dancing With The Stars | 74 |
| Meeting Of The Moms | 78 |
| To The Brothers | 81 |
| Buried Alive | 83 |
| Death Is Knocking | 85 |
| If They Are Hungry Feed Them | 89 |
| If The Shoe Fits | 91 |
| Politically Speaking | 94 |
| Mission Impossible | 96 |
| My Lord | 98 |
| I'm Not Going Back | 101 |
| My Four Sons | 103 |
| Spare Change | 104 |
| Monster On A Leash | 106 |
| High Hopes | 109 |
| The Audition | 113 |
| The Position | 116 |
| 911 Emergency Hotline! | 119 |
| Person In The Mirror | 120 |
| True Confession | 121 |
| There Go I | 123 |
| I'm Pregnant | 125 |
| One Life To Live | 127 |
| Addiction Stole My Child | 128 |
| The Party Is Over | 130 |
| The Choices We Make | 132 |
| Showing Up For Life | 135 |
| Small Beginnings | 137 |
| The Blame Game | 139 |
| One String | 140 |
| My Addiction | 142 |
| A Poet's Perspective | 143 |
| Earth To Men | 145 |
| But God | 147 |
| Life's Bully | 149 |
| Had A Little Talk With Jesus | 150 |
| A Friend Till The End | 152 |
| The Good Old Days | 154 |

| | |
|---|---|
| I Got Robbed | 156 |
| Looking For An Angel | 157 |
| Officer | 158 |
| Stark Naked | 160 |
| Under The Sky | 162 |
| What If? | 164 |
| In A While | 166 |
| Bootlickers | 167 |
| Shakazulu Where Are You | 169 |
| The War Outside | 171 |
| A Letter To Our Ancestors | 173 |
| Shower Power | 175 |
| Who Is That Woman? | 177 |
| The Same Boat | 179 |
| Holy Ground | 182 |
| I Swear | 183 |
| Whose Child | 185 |
| The Family Truce | 187 |
| Alzheimer's Speaks!! | 188 |
| Pride And Prejudice | 190 |
| Main Line | 192 |
| What If | 194 |
| The Other Woman | 196 |
| The Boogie Man | 197 |
| This Poem | 199 |
| On His Way!!! | 201 |
| A Gentle Giant | 203 |
| You'r Angel | 205 |
| My Mind | 206 |
| Pretty In Pink | 208 |
| Sister With A New Attitude | 210 |
| Super Hero | 211 |
| The War | 213 |
| The Dining Room | 215 |
| The Care Giver | 216 |
| I Too Know Why The Caged Bird Sings | 218 |

# INTRODUCTION

Through my imagery style poetry I believe that God has given me a gift to create artistic expressions that produces a spiritual response of strength and inspiration in others, who are spiritually broken. Some of my verses resonate with the pain, despair and aspirations of those who live in neighborhoods where murder, addiction, sexual abuse and grinding poverty are everyday facts of life.

For those who don't live there, the 'hood is a far off place. Many witness these atrocities over the internet or on TV. My hope is that my poetry will give readers a window into a world where people are crying out for help, also recognizing that even in the mist of tragedies and despair there is still good that transpires in our communities.

I didn't learn my craft in a rarified grove of academe. Terms such as iambic pentameter and metonymy don't trip off my tongue. As a middle child growing up with three brothers and five sisters, we all attended Williams Temple Church in Ansonia CT. There, gospel songs inspired me. At school, I developed an early passion for poetry. I'd stand in front of the class reciting the works of Robert Frost and Edgar Allen Poe because I loved to hear the sounds of alliteration, repetition and rhyme. Everything in life turned into a poem for me.

Friends call me Sister Deborah, not only as a spiritual designation but also because it is my performance name in the poetry arena. One of my accomplishments that gives me great satisfaction is stepping out on faith and creating S.W.A.N.A. This support group brings me in close contact with women who are struggling in many areas of their life's. Of course money would be a blessing to all, but more than that people need to feel secure and cared about. They want safe policing, education and mentoring for their children, jobs that pay a decent wage and to know that their issues and concerns are not last on a very, very long list.

I believe that because of my own past substance abuse issues and ongoing recovery I have been assigned to share hope with others. I have recited my poems at jails, festivals, churches, rehab centers and town greens—even city buses. My poetry describes what the heart sees and feels. It touches on love, betrayal, injustice, despair, racism, gun violence, mental illness, child abuse, substance abuse, recovery, spiritual deliverance domestic violence, unemployment and recidivism.

I am the mother of five beautiful children—four sons and one daughter—who are often the ones who inspire me to write. I recently took a trip to South Africa where the country and the people inspired me to write even more.

This is the first time my poems have been collected in a book. What I want people to take away with them after reading my verses is the fact that everybody goes through rough patches in life—some rougher than others. Through these times, I encourage everyone to hold on to God's unchanging hand and to remember that when we are weak, God is still yet STRONG.

Sister Deborah Elmore

# THE JOURNEY

This is the route I traveled
and where God has brought me from.
Yes . . . very troubled waters
before victory was won.

I started out near the lake of
Depression
before I got to the river of tears.
This is where the enemy had me
embarked
In a thunderstorm of fear.

I travelled high to the mountain of sorrow.
For I had no faith in the word
tomorrow.

Miraculously his majesty heard me
calling out
from the valley of death
from the valley of doubt.

Here the Lord came and rescued me.
Yes, deliverance out of bondage
Is what he did for me.

I now reside on the island of hope
with many other believers
who once could not cope.

# BORN AGAIN

Remove the lipstick
the tight jeans,
and the makeup too.

You're my daughter,
my special child,
and my grace is sufficient for you.

No longer are you to hide your beauty
under a colorful mask.
Because only the things, that are done in my name
have the stamina to last.

No longer are you to use your vessel
as a dumping ground for waste.
I've got bigger plans for you my daughter
and again it deals with my grace.

The men that I have allowed
to wreck havoc in your life,
Wipe your tears,
cry no more,
for no longer can they entice.

The expensive jewelry,
the fancy cars,
and all of the finest clothes,
are material things that you never really needed
for your victory I have aligned in gold.

Before I could not use you
because you allowed the things of this world
to stand in my way,
but now that I have taught you humility
I work through you every day.

You are now my humble servant,
one of my many vessels on this earth.
When I send you out into the vineyard,
your job, your assignment is to poetically
reach out to those who hurt.

Yet, still you have some glitches,
small things I have observed,
like mumbling and complaining,
sometimes forgetting who you serve.

Nevertheless,
all these things will come to pass
and I will grant you the desires of your heart,
as you spend more time in my word.

Remember to look to the hills
from which comes your help.
for your help, my daughter, cometh from the Lord.

You have been born again!!

# TEN DOLLARS

**$10.00 sold!**
is how I lost my soul.
I stepped off the narrow
and chose the broad unrighteous road.
I thought I was cool,
I thought I was hip,
but let me break it down to you
about this life-altering trip.

**Ten dollars** for a lifetime of tears.
That doesn't sound quite reasonable.
It certainly doesn't sound quite fair.
But this is how the enemy works
when he whispers sweet nothings in your ear.
I'll never forget his words
because I've cried a blood river of tears.

When the enemy comes after you,
he comes after you quick.
Before you blink your eye
you're already in a ditch.
Lost my kids,
my home,
my two cars,
and everything else I owned,
while Satan sat back and watched
from his dark uncompassionate throne.
My life now existed only in the twilight zone.
**Ten dollars**
and my life is a mess,
no food,
no money,
not even a decent dress.

What happened to me?
Where did I go?
I was so desperate; hungry for love,
that I allowed Satan to convince me
to take a job
working on the low
Jesus, Father, God please help me,
I cried out from the deep down below.

I now existed in a scary place,
one with no color,
one with no face.
All the enemy left me with was shame and disgrace.

But you know what everybody!
I had one thing left.
It was buried deep down,
tucked away under the left side of my breast.
It was hidden in a crease where only
the savior could see that I was crying inside and that I saw no relief.

But what I had hiding there was a tiny mustard seed.
So, I'm here to tell the drug addicted-the prostitute-the HIV infected the homeless,
and the jobless that faith is all you need.

Use your next $10.00 to sow your seed!!!!!

# DRESSING UP MY PAIN

Ladies I'm still struggling to squeeze into my favorite blue dress,
top half so tight that it's compressing my breast.
You know the one with the zipper that gives me a sharp pain down the side,
all because I still want to dance and be the exact same size.
Sixty pounds later the devil is a liar.
It seems like it was only yesterday
I was twenty, beautiful and a dashing size five.

Not a care, not a bill or a worry in the world,
just me and my Camaro coasting down the highway
giving life a twirl.

Well, the twirl is over; it actually ended twenty years ago,
but I'm still stuck on the highway
with nowhere to go.
I'm out of gas and my engine light is on.
I know that I need a tune up
but my get up and go is gone.

I'm wearing my pretty blue shoes
with the matching blue hat and gloves.
Blue is my favorite color because blue reminds me of love.

Ouch! These shoes are really pinching.
On my face I hope it doesn't show
that my blue shoes no longer fit either,
and that they have actually lost their soles.
I'm still gonna wear these shoes
because no one has to know
that on this dark highway I don't want my wrinkles
or grey hairs to show.
I don't want anyone to see my belly roll
or the cold hard fact that I have simply grown old.

I want to ride from my pain and disguise my hurt.
So I continue to squeeze into this same blue dress,
trying hard to cover up my hurt.

# JESUS IS GONNA GET YOU

Why?

You have the audacity to ask
because you sat there and did nothing
instead of getting up off your ass.
You just sat there and watched while his people were treated wrong.
You didn't lift a finger or bother to listen to their song

Why?

Because you say that you've heard it
time and time again.
Just imagine if
God treated you this way.
You'd be no better off then them.

Why?

Because in God's eyes, sin is sin.
They just don't have the finances
to cover where they've been.

There will always be poor people,
the same as there will always be rich.
But two wrongs don't make a right
leaving you both in the same ditch.

You know that it's not right,
treating the poor this way.
But all you did was turn your head
and walk the other way.
You could have spoken out,
intervened in some small way.
You could have said "don't hang the poor guy!"
For God's sake I've got plenty, I'll pay!
But you didn't. You sat there and watched them drag
that poor guy away.

When God does ask you,
what honor you did with the life he gave to you,
what in the world are you gonna say?

Jesus is gonna get you.

# THE FIGHT

Anybody here want to see a good fight,
one where hitting below the belt is devastatingly right?
Eye gauging, ear biting
nothing is left concealed.
This fighter has no conscience.
He'll tear your heart into shreds.
He won't stop kicking you
until all of your dreams are dead.

She has been your worst enemy
for quite a number of years.
she'll laugh right in your face
while you cry a river of tears.

I'm sure each of you know this fighter
because this fight is between you and you.
You are your own worst enemy
and this is why you always lose.
Stop beating on yourself and give yourself a break.
So what if you didn't make it on time.
At least you showed up,
did your part
and stepped up to the plate.

So you didn't get the outfit or the latest hairdo.
You still came as your authentic self.
Unlike others, you came as the real you.
You say your car is not brand new.
Well, at least its getting you from point a-z
you could be stuck in another country.
Begging, crying out for mercy.

Most of us don't know what it is
to have absolutely nothing, zero to eat.
So let us all be grateful to God and humbly take a seat.

# THE WAR ZONE

In-coming!!!!!!!!!!!!!!!!!!!!!!!!!!!!!!!
everybody hit the deck

Some of us have already gotten wounded,
others not yet.
Gunfire-bullets and fights all the time.
drug-selling drug-doing
here there is no peace of mind.
Family members fighting
pit bulls biting—many enemy sightings.

Here there is friendly fire
your own brother
your own sister
your own uncle
stone cold liars.

The teens don't listen.
They don't believe they are in harms way.
They can't figure out for the love of money
that the men in the blue suits will come
and gladly haul their butts away.
not just for an hour or two,
but for a million days.
Shackle and chain you just like a slave.

They can't hear their mamas crying
pleading for them to leave Satan's work alone,
all they can hear is that familiar chirp
(where you at?)
and those ridiculous ring tones.

Thirty days on guard duty
no rest or any sleep.
I'm afraid that the enemy will launch a full attack
and take out my troops if I enjoy the luxury of falling asleep.

Thank God for the prayer line
many nights I'm able to tap in and get through.
Send out an S.O.S.
to other soldiers who are fighting the same war
who are being viscously attacked too.

Again I live in the war zone
but today I'm going out.
Things can't be no worst <u>outside</u>
than they are in my own damn house
over and out!

# COKE ADDICT

Hi everybody.
my name is—
and I am
a struggling coke addict.
I tried my best to kick it
but this is a tough one
this is a bad . . . habit.

The first thing my sponsor says
is that I need to admit.
But you see I find those words quite difficult (my ego and all)
because I thought for sure
I was big enough, intelligent enough, strong enough, tough enough
to just up and quit.

How could I allow something like this to hold me down
wake me up in the wee hours of the night
and demand I drive across town.

Even when I'm at work
I swear I can hear it calling out to me.
"meet me over at the canteens so that I can set you free."
Friends and co-workers are totally sick of me.
They tell me that I've been saying the same two words
( I and quit) since 2003. 11 years of the same misery
even my little niece says
Auntie . . . . why don't you just make a CD?

Anyways, I've started using the harm reduction model.
by lessening my use everyday.
I've even sunk to a different brand
Pepsi-Mountain Dew
but I still find it hard to stay away.

I've tried little quotes
like 'one day at a time'
but I'm telling you I'm hooked on this soda
and I'm ready to loose my mind.

Somebody!
anybody!
please help me to pray
that I can muster up enough courage
to just say no to this addiction
and walk the heck away.

# WHO'S RUNNING THE CIRCUS?

Because there is no one at the gate
I went to ask the ticket booth lady
but it appears she's running late.

I mean,
here there are no tigers and bears,
only real human beings crying tear after heart broken tear.
The elephants don't have big ears
and the lady behind the curtain never disappeared.

Instead of lions there are real people jumping through hoops
trying to make a living without real loot.

Children walking the tight rope of life
with no real hope or meaning of what's right.

People are juggling bills
instead of juggling balls.
Teenagers answering the internet
instead of their parents' call.

Again I ask
Who is running this circus?
because to them this is really a big joke.

With no concern for life
children or elderly folks,
the man with two faces
turned out to be my friend.
Isn't that funny
because he always kept a grin.

Even the cotton candy had a strange taste.
I found out later in the emergency room
that it was actually mixed and laced.

I should never have come to this circus
I was better off at home
watching my old black and white TV
and enjoying real popcorn.
Who the heck is running this circus?

# DIFFERENT

I will not
I shall not
apologize for being me.

I am unique
different
simply one of a kind.
No longer lost
no longer blind.

I stand before you with God in my heart
and the kingdom on my mind.

Like each of you my DNA is different
unlike anybody else.
When God fashioned and formed me
He didn't put the mold back on the shelf.
He tossed it
broke it
threw it far into the sea,
because I'm not to be like you
and you're not to be like me.
Some say I'm peculiar
some say she's odd.
It really doesn't' matter
because it's all about God

You see he fashioned and formed me
for his Glory!!!!!!!!!!!!

# I FOUND ME

You are not going to believe where I was at.
after twenty years of searching
I came from behind the tracks.
I was covered with dust from head to toe.
I was tucked down the bottom rails
where no one would know.
The little light that God gave to me
was unable to shine.
because someone threw a blanket over me
in a wicked attempt for me to loose my mind
whoever it was I know Satan was behind.

I was made to feel like a bird with a broken wing
a can with a dent
a penny with a hole in it
a tie rod that was bent.
All because I would not consent.

God had done a new thing
separating me from man.
No longer was I
to worry about foolishness
time for me to stand.

# HURT BY THE CHURCH

Hurt by the church
and I'm not going back.
I thought I was hurt before I came in,
but this is a wound
a real gusher
big enough to send me
back out in the world again.

I was only there for a little while
before I noticed some things just were not right
what I saw
what I observed was Christians judging Christians
a word I just learned in bible study
last Wednesday night.
I believe the meaning of this action
is called back bite.

Lord have mercy
where is everybody's light?
I've come in out of darkness
and I need spiritual sight
not eyes rolling
heads bobbing
notes being slid up under the pews
I need to see some true God fearing Christians
the kind that God can use.

Remember that I'm just a baby
with this thing called born again.
I don't exactly understand how it all takes place
but for the love of God I want to win.
Besides, anything is better
than living a life full of miserable sin.
I've been beat by my mother
and violated by my dad,
the two people I should have been able to trust
in this world have made me so devastatingly sad.
The last thing I need to think now
is that even church people are bad.

You see the church is my only hope.
If you take that away
I just as well go back to getting high
shooting dope.
Because the only thing you've done
was shorten the noose and tighten up the rope.

Hurt by the church.

# HOLLA BACK!!!

I heard that you holler at you mother
what a doggone, disgusting shame.
After carrying you for nine months,
then enduring hours of hard labor pain.
She was the first person
to kiss you
to welcome you into this world.

She was the first person to love you and give you your first baby toy
the very first person to wipe your tears
and let you know she would always love you and that she would always
care.

Yeah . . . . but life has not been perfect.
God knows she made her share of mistakes.
You didn't come with a handbook
nothing that she could relate.
Plus mom had her own troubles
in this world no one escapes.
Jobs, heartaches, bills
so mom did the best she could
if she could have gave you the world
you know that she would.

There's something called a fine line
it's a mutual line of respect.
You dare not cross it at any time
or from your own child you will one day get

disrespect
cussed at
and basically abused,
all because you didn't follow
God's commandment, his rule.

Honor Thy Mother and Father

and don't ever Holla back!!!!!

# THE TRUTH

How many of you know that the truth is like a short blanket
if you pull it over your shoulders
your feet will stick out.
If you try to cover your feet, then your shoulders will be out.

Does anybody have a tissue I can use?
because I'm about to tell the truth
I hope nobody laughs at me,
but God told me to shame the devil.

He told me to let this burden loose.
I've been wearing this phony smile
backed up by praise the lord
I haven't been on my knees in two years
and God only knows the whereabouts of my sword
the last time I saw it was somewhere under the bed
dusty disheveled
I can't even tell you the last scripture I read.

Anyways, I've been allowing Satan to have his way.
He's been whispering sweet nothings in my ear each and every day.
He been telling me that I am unblessed poor and that's the way I'm
gonna stay.
He's been using my own children against me
so I live in a world of dismay.

During my time of deep depression last year
the enemy took it upon himself to move into my head.
Just set up camp
kicked over my little bit of faith and blew out my God given lamp.
He wasn't invited.
He wasn't welcome
but he knew that I was no longer using my shield.

He knew that I had assumed the position of giving up and that I would soon yield.
he told me to start back playing Lotto
because this was truly the only way
for me to pay the bills.

# IF PEOPLE TOLD THE TRUTH

(First scenario)
Good Morning Sister Jones
How are you today?
Highly favored and sanctified.
Filled with the Holy Ghost,
too anointed to be disappointed.
And to Blessed to be stressed!

(Second scenario)
Good Morning Sister Jones
How are you today?
To be honest with you my back is hurting and the pain in
my knees just won't go away.

Well how is the job going?
You've been there for over twenty years.
I actually got laid off two years ago
and my life has been reduced to tears.

They don't want to give me my pension
and I have depleted my 4012k.
I'm living off of my savings and soon that too will go away.
No one is willing to hire me
because all they can see is my grey.
I worked hard all of my life
and it really bothers me to be ignored, and defined this way.

(My Lord, My Lord)

Well what about the kids?
They must all be grown by now.
Well . . . . Johnny is in jail
and Thomas is on the run.
Plus . . . I'm raising my four Grandkids until my daughters fight is won.
I'm just waiting for the storms in my life to pass
So that I can once again see the sun.

# THE WILDERNESS

Has anybody here ever had a wilderness experience?
The kind that makes you feel like your all alone,
the kind where you can't find your way out of your troubles and all you
can do is moan.

It's times like this when the enemy tries his best to convinces you
that the wilderness is now your permanent new home
dark, scary and a zillion miles from God's throne.

The wilderness is a cold place
your whole life is frozen over
no amount of blankets or quilts
can replace.

Every tree looks the same
every branch resembles pain
your heart is frostbitten
and you're starting to feel insane.

For weeks you've been walking in circles
with no relief in sight
all because you insist on using your own puny strength
instead of God's all-powerful might.

If you would only stop murmuring and complaining
you would be able to see the light.
It's dim now but if you would just hold on
the light will get bright.

# LIFE'S LESSONS

I received some bad news today
that a friend of mine
an old buddy had quietly passed away.
I was shocked, devastated, wounded to say the least.
when I suppose I should just be grateful
that she finally made her peace.

But no, I'm upset
because I didn't say good-bye
but then again I had all year to pick up the telephone
and say "Hi."

Now I want to send flowers
but too late.
She'll never smell
she'll never know that I thought she was a great person
because I never took the time out to tell.

Too busy
other things on my mind.
Now I sit in a world of grief
wishing I could turn back the hands of time.

This is one of life's lessons
regretfully one that we all must learn.
If you love, care, or respect anyone
you must honestly voice your concern.

Sometimes in life we get angry
sometimes we get mad.
Sometimes we say things from our mouths
that we wish we never had.
Sometimes we allow the little things in life
make us forget about all the good times that we've had.

Right now my heart is troubled
but I'll keep my head up high
the friend I knew
wouldn't want me to feel sad and she certainly wouldn't want me to cry.

She would want me to pass this lesson on
to the next person
before any more loved ones die.

Sometimes we just have to speak up
and push foolish pride aside.

# ROUND TWO

At this corner of the ring ladies and gentlemen we have Crystal Meth.
She is a seductive, lethal, powerful highly addictive contender
that will transform your entire life into a mess.

At the other end of the ring
we have Ivy league college graduate Seth.
Born and raised in the better part of Connecticut
ninety-eight pounds soaking wet.
He's been fighting this fight for over four years
his parents can no longer afford his habit
and have been reduced to tears.

Now Crystal is quicker, colorless and odorless
always sending a sharp right upper cut.

So mentally and physically challenging
that the first round
usually lands Seth on his butt.

But Seth is in denial
and actually believes he can take Crystal on
just one more time.
He does not see that he is hallucinating again
and that he is actually out of his mind.

There goes the bell
Seth is flying high
but again Crystal is in pure form
giving her the stamina, the ability
to last all night long.

For anyone crazy enough to step into the ring
not only am I a sports announcer
but I've taken a few classes
and I've studied up on a few things.

Like how Crystal Meth can cause rapid heartbeat
increased blood pressure
and damage blood vessels to the brain.

How she can produce psychotic episodes
weeks, months, or even years after you have broken up with her
and left the game.
How she can contribute to pneumonia, tuberculosis
hepatitis B and C eventually liver and kidney disease.

Whether you
Huff her
Puff her
Sniff her
or inject her
when you step into the ring with Crystal
you are definitely out of your league.

Again take it from your announcer
and walk away from Crystal.
She's one bad seed.

# CANNING

A way of life
many see it as unproductive
almost repulsive
because in their minds
they cannot fathom the canner's plight.

They can no way imagine
this clangy carriage full of empty bottles and cans
being a lifestyle for anyone
let alone a grown woman or man.

They say
"What in the world would make a person
start picking up cans and live without a home?"
I say
Since we don't know this individual's whole story,
we should put down our sticks and stones.

Understand that all man's spiritual eyes are not open
so they are unable to see
that this is the canner's life
this is now his identity
the only treasure he claims in this world
this rusty old carriage to him is a pearl.

So don't look down
make snide remarks
or turn your head up high.
Don't laugh
snicker
if anything, you should try

to help this person, less fortunate than you
because if not for the grace of God
this really could be you or a family member
broken, homeless without any shoes.

The canner minds his own business
just goes about his merry way
happy as a pig in mess
and this small happiness you want to take away.

I know people who have an abundance of material things
money to throw away
but they won't offer you a slice of pie
because they feel that they are much better
and that they too sit high.
But you must keep in mind that only God sits on high
and looks down low
to make sure that the poor and the homeless
have somewhere to go
that someone would lend a helping hand
by showing kindness to all man.

Remember the only time we should look down on
anyone is when we are reaching down to help them up
this way we won't forget to be grateful
for the way life's pie was cut.

# INVISIBLE

Invisible man
invisible woman
exactly who are these people
that the world cannot see?
They can't hear their agonizing screams
or empathize with their needs.

They're my neighbors
my co-workers
my colleagues
my friends
they're people who work hard everyday
to make an honest living
but cannot meet their ends.

They are those on fixed income
who simply don't have any more.
They're people who don't share the luxury
of a second trip to the grocery store.

You say feed the hungry
the homeless
and clothe the poor.
Well we're one step behind
because we too need more.

Between school
work and raising the kids,
How much more do you want
one person to give?
Doctors, dentists, community affairs
now jury duty
I'm reduced to tears.
Get a second job is that what you say
if I stretch my life any further
they'll be no need for more pay.

A workman is always worth
their weight in gold
but you can't squeeze a rusty dime
from an empty soul.

# NIKKA

Fifty years of living on this vast planet earth
this is my home
my place of residence
the natural place of my birth.

I know that racism, criticism,
cynicism
is still yet sadly alive
but never in my entire life
was I taken by such total surprise
33 thousand feet up in the friendly skies.

I was
shocked
appalled
outraged
offended to say the least.
Now I'm left wondering
about the mark of the beast.

I now had mixed feelings
that were flying off the chart
because her words had the magnitude
to break down my heart.

A baby
a toddler
a beautiful little girl
with big brown eyes
and a head full of curls
laughing and giggling and having innocent fun.
She had no idea that she had just shot me with a gun.

She was someone who knew nothing about life
or the destruction racism plays in our world.
She was someone who knew nothing about the tongue being used as a
dangerous weapon when lashed out and hurled.
The bible tells us that out of the mouths of babes
do we learn.
Well let me tell you my story
and how words truly do burn.

Nika-nika-nika is the word she used for me
over and over every time she turned around in her seat.
Taught this destructive language
before the tender age of three.

I was hurt
angry mad and sad all at the same time
but I had to collect my emotions
and keep my dignity in line.

We have to teach our children to love not to hate
because of teachings like that
no one will make it to the gate.

I am not a nigger
actually I am one of God's greats.
He does not make junk
and he does not make mistakes.

Nikka

# GOD IS CALLING

God calls the young because they are strong
God calls the old because they know the way
but I'm looking at some of the older generation
who have totally gone astray.

You cannot teach God's children
by living and acting this way.
When you yourself don't take the time
to spend with God and pray.

Some of you elders are totally out of place
whore mugging, drugging
it's a downright disgrace.
God has been calling for you to pull yourselves
together and stand in your rightful place.
Talk about Sodom and Gomorra
everybody sinning and doing their own thing.
How can we guide the children?
How can freedom ever ring?

Their pants are hanging
and so are yours.
Your skirt is too tight
just like hers.
You don't work.
Why should they?
Like you
video games
is what they choose to play.

He sends the rainbow to remind us
that he won't flood the earth again.
But prepare yourself for the fire and
brimstone
if you don't turn from your wicked sins

God is calling!!!!!!!!!!!!!!!!

# THE WHITE HOUSE

From the *out* house
to the White House
that's how far our people have come.
Many of them were murdered
Some simply passed away
still yet clinging to the promise
that by-and-by we would all see this day.

On November 4, 2008 thousands gathered for a moment in time
that would forever count and forever be great!
I witnessed a flood of people
crying a river of tears.
People of all colors and cultures
united to watch and hear.

President Elect Obama!!!!!!!!!!!!!!!!!!!!!!!!!
were the words that rang in our ears.
It was like music
the sweet taste of honey
a mother kissing her baby's tears.

I felt Martin Luther King's hand on my shoulder
saw Rosa Parks taking her seat
that church in Alabama go up in flames
Harriet Tubman sigh a sound of relief.
I heard thousands of footsteps
marching through Birmingham.
I heard Kunta Kinte tell his master
that he too is a man.
I saw the North Star give off a great shine.
I felt my heart skip a beat
then fall back in line.

I felt victory conquer oppression for the very first time.
Much more than that, it was like a million people crossed their fingers
and said the same prayer at the very same time.
Please GOD, whatever happens just let this election be fair.
You would think that God himself stopped by
to remind us that he still cares.

Many of our ancestors helped build the White House,
worked, painted, cooked and
cleaned the White House,
It is merely karma that we finally
take a seat in the *White House.*

This Poem is Dedicated to the President of the United States
Mr Barak Obama for a Job Well Done!

# BUT GOD

I spent the night with Jesus.
He held me in his arms.
He told me to stop shivering and crying
because he would calm the storm.
He reminded me that he loves me
and that he would keep me warm.

I said, *But God* there's a blizzard
going on inside of me.

He told me, Daughter just weather the storm
and I will set you free.
There are just some things that you must go through
so that the world can see you and me.

*But God* my heart is broken
and its more than I can bare.

Need I remind you again my child
that I love you and that I care.
I know this is this is a tough one
but I gave you my word a long time ago.
Listen to me as I direct your path
and I will show you which way to go.

Do not get discouraged
for the things you do not see.
Do not allow intimidation
to pass your way
To you there is a prophecy.

In time things will begin to unfold
right before your eyes.
The treasures I have stored up for you
will embrace your very soul.

But God

# SEARCHING

I bet your all wondering what it is I'm looking for.
I have been searching diligently
because this particular item cannot be purchased
at any store.

Oh there is no amount of money
that can buy this back for me.
it was one of a kind
tailored real fine
fit like a glove you see.
I have been searching relentlessly
I mean high and low
if only I could find it
no telling how far I could go.

I could probably climb mountains
Touch every cloud n the sky
Walk amongst the biggest giants
and not once question why.

if I could just find it
no doubt I would be alright.

Has anyone here guessed it?
that's right! It's my self esteem
Without it I can't stand tall
Without it I will always lean.
I'll lean on other people
I'll always have an excuse.
I won't try to help my own self out
I'll settle for the life of a recluse.

Actually it was stolen
by someone that I trusted in a long time ago
So today trust is a big issue for me
I don't want anyone to try and befriend me
or go beyond my set boundaries.

By now some of you have already guessed it.
It's my own dark, ugly secret wound.

That's right I've been molested.

# EIGHTEEN WITH A BULLET

Son
I know that you may not understand this
(but don't do it).
You can't see the impact that this bullet will have on your life
the pain, the remorse the sorrow, past tonight.
Please don't allow anger to have it's way
grab a hold of your teen-hood and walk the heck away
Violence is never the answer on any given day.

You're eighteen with a bullet.

You see anger won't allow you
to focus or think
about your family and friends
people with whom you are linked.
People who will miss your smile every night and everyday.
Son, if you pull that trigger
the men in blue
will shackle, chain, cuff and most likely beat the hell out of you.

You're eighteen with a bullet.

Listen every neighborhood has a neighborhood mom
someone to listen and attempt to keep the neighborhood kids calm
She's that one that they call Ma Dukes.

She the one who will make sure that every kid on the block has food.
She is the same one to encourage you to take your butt to school.
She's the one to insist you can make it when others call you a fool.

You're eighteen with a bullet
Listen to your elders son
and PLEASE . . . . . don't do it.

# THE ROLE MODEL

My Role Model
My Mentor
Looks just like me.
a bit older
a bit wiser
but in him I see me
Tall dark and handsome
with his pants down to his knees.

He drinks and he does drugs
half the day and half the night,
then he wants to yell at me
when mom says I am not acting right.
What a joke
my mentor, my so called Dad, living a double life.

How do you think I feel
when I see a drug deal
go down between him and my friend?
This is a movie stuck in my head
It plays every night before I go to bed
Damn! Sometimes I wish he were dead
I wish he was a real teacher
but he's a hypocrite instead.

It kills me when he starts to yell
like I'm really suppose to follow him
staggering through the gates of hell.

My friend knows that he should not sell
but his role model
the man that he has always looked up to
is dictating to him from a cell.
He writes my friend weekly, but only to yell
send more money and keep up the sales
What kind of roll model is that?

Is it any wonder the dysfunction that goes on in the 'hood
when kids are raising kids the way parents should.
When young boys and girls are parents at an early age
they have no real concept of life just a broken gage
so what do we do as a community
just turn the page.

People cannot teach
what they do not know
and like a domino affect
they can't articulate where it is they want to go
Simply because they had no one to show.

God meant for man to be the head and not the tail
to be the back bone and not the wish bone
that many women/mothers wish they had.
To take care of the family
and be the roll model in the home
not leave her with a bunch of kids
and decide he wants to roam.

Without the real head
A house could never be a home
only a place that resembles the twilight zone
Remember everyone that this is only a poem
only a poem
only a poem . . . .
only a poem.

# THIS IS NOT MY DAUGHTER

This is not my daughter who resides with me.
This is a stranger
nowhere near the daughter I raised.
this person bites and growls
sometimes throws fits of rage.

She's got the right address
and the proper ID
but I tell you this is not my daughter living with me.

My daughter had silk skin
and beautiful curly hair
well mannered
well groomed
and about others she always cared.

My real daughter would never raise her hand to me
Demand money and take authority
I want this person out of my house
out of my jewelry box
and off of my couch
Sometimes I'm temped to call the police on her
but my heart always screams ouch!

I asked her who are you just the other day.
She looked at me and answered,
I'm your daughter Mom. Just continue to pray.
Don't give up all hope on me.
I too have been praying for God to set me free
to get this ugly gorilla off of my back
so that I can regroup and get my life back on track.

For months I have been in denial
not wanting family and friends to know
but denial has taken over my life
and now this stranger and denial run the entire show.

Well do you know what denial?
I want my life back
I want my beautiful daughter
and I want you to get up and pack.

My daughter is now in recovery
where she is getting her life back
and taking authority.

She is coming out of darkness and into the marvelous light
she is now in rehab plus attending church regaining back her sight.
She is learning how to stand and walk again
My daughter is finally excepting the fact
that she was not born to loose
but to win.

# THE BIG DOGS

What a greedy, selfish, uncaring pack
These well groomed dogs are viscous man eaters
and compassion they totally lack.

People who have no health insurance seem to be their greatest snack.
These money hungry canines will tear the shirt off of a baby's back.
They choose to rip every piece of meat off the bone
Its merely business a profit to them, when they hear the poor man moan.

These big dogs live in beautiful dog houses
driveways aligned in gold.
Each brick represents someone with no health insurance soul.
These dogs eat only the best of kibbles and bits
a little bit of you and a little bit of me.
Our agony over health insurance
they refuse to except or see.

I went to a long awaited doctor appointment the other day.
When my name was called, they informed me that they could not see me today.
I tried to explain that my pain was in no better way.
She turned to the computer and said sorry but you have no medical to pay.
I cried that I waited four months to be seen
and that the pain in my stomach was awfully mean.

She explained that the only other way to be seen
was if I had papers with dead presidents on green.
If not step aside so that someone with real health insurance could be seen
I simply told her that I had no money to pay
I'm now collecting unemployment and went on my way.

I called the department of social services
ten times that day
and pleaded my case
to an answering machine that had no face.

The next morning I got up bright and early
I was on my way
to speak to a worker
and have my say.

Again I waited in line
only to be told
that I could not see my worker
and that the computers were froze.
She simply directed me to the wall phone
and again I stayed on hold
Next I heard a loud bark
No it was more like a growl
It was actually the head supervisor throwing me a white towel.

# THE BRICK

Hit in the face with a brick
never seen it coming
unprepared for this.

My so-called friend
was hiding it right behind his back
kept it tucked away for years
before laying me out flat.

He walked with me
he talked with me
but he never, never said
watch out friend
duck
because I plan to knock off your head.
I plan to hit you so hard
that you will never forget that you knew me
and that our entire relationship was a farce.

Damn!
he could have used a pebble.
Shit he could have used a rock
But my so-called friend chose a brick
so that when I went down
he could continue to kick.
He threw the brick so hard
and with such force
that it knocked me off my feet
traveled to my heart
and left me without speech
I was so left in a daze that I couldn't sleep for weeks.

People tried to warn me
your friend is up to no good
but I wouldn't listen
because I never thought he could.

Bite the hand that fed him
took him in out of the cold
share my last penny
and always tried to warm his soul.

No point in complaining
because this is what you get
when family and friends
try to warn you
about the wolf in sheep's clothing
before the brick hits.

# **NEVER CAME HOME**

My son went away to Vietnam
A young man, handsome,
well-spoken and filled with charm
He would have been any mothers pride and joy
My son was a solider in the United States Army
No longer a boy.

I have some pictures of my son when he was around three
memoirs
my fondest memories of him and me
He would play on the kitchen floor for hour
with his plastic solders and say Mom look at me!
When I grow up I'm gonna be a solider one day
I'm gonna fight for our country
and be all I can be
Mom
I'm gonna make you and Dad proud of me.

He was as cute as a button
my son
my first baby
I tell you the truth
he meant the world to me.

So now my son is in Vietnam
fighting little people that we call conges
for my son this is more than the kitchen floor
theses soiled fight back
this is real war.

guns, grenades bombs blood and guts
if you lived this horrific life everyday
would people call you nuts.

Well, my son has been home now
for over twenty years
He clings to an invisible riffle
and his eyes in a blank stare
I still try to hug him and kiss him
but my son is not there
sometimes he thinks that I am the enemy
and at me his eyes will flare.
He often recites his dog tag number to me
a piece of tin with numbers engraved on it
is all that I can see
like a badge of honor repetitiously
his name his number and the life he'll never see.

Your left
Your left
Your left right left.
That's right my son left over twenty years ago
and he never really came home
not the boy I raised who now lives in the twilight zone.

Not the one on patrol
guarding the bathroom door
the refrigerator
and the couch
not the one that retreats to the basement bunker every night
and causes my heart to scream ouch!!

I just want my son to know
that a mother's love
has the strength and the fortitude to keep
the lamp burning until her child comes home.
God will set the time
and then God will set the tone
one way or another
in this life or the next
my son is coming home.

# WHERE'S OUR PARTY?

Where is our homecoming party
and where is our parade?
Why aren't all of the balloons blown up
Like many of our arms and legs.

I cannot hear the horn section
when I am cold and in my grave
I would like to have my flowers now
today!
for living a life that was brave.

Where is my apartment
No my house?
Why am I homeless and on the streets?
What happened to taking care of your own
or was that just a dream until we got home
its ironic because I thought I just left
the twilight zone.

Land of the brave
home of the free
All I'm asking is that you keep up your end of the bargain
and take good care of me and my buddies, my comrades, my friends
You see we were honest and made a pact for life
friends till the end.

I remember enlisting in the army
My parents so proud of me
strong handsome and determined
I was just twenty-three
my parents did not have a clue
as to where they were sending me
and what I was commanded to do.

I really don't care to talk about it
all the things I seen and did.
You won't understand that I'm just a man
and all I wanted to do was get back home and live
Talk about a real fight for life
My salute to the soldiers who go back twice

**Special high salute to the soldiers who have given their life.**

# DANCING WITH THE STARS

***A tribute to Michael Jackson***

Who really killed Michael Jackson?

Was what the world wanted to know.
Well I've done some research.
I even searched the scriptures
and this is how it goes
you did it
you did it
I did
we all did it
if . . . . .
the honest to God truth
be told.

Yes, we killed him when we kept silent
when he was being burned at the stake
Not enough of us stood up to shout ***beat it!***
this is horrific mistake
this man is not a monster
this man is one of Gods Greats.

A beautiful star sent to earth
to so brilliantly shine
Michael lit up the entire world
with his Mega talent and his nature of being kind.

The forensics report speaks volumes
but the spiritual facts determined that Michael was long gone
before that administer drug.
He died because many of his longtime fans
Hypocrites
nay sayers
his own people
stopped giving him a hug.
When he got into trouble many turned their backs
quick to believe the tabloids
and shut off the life saving blood.

Detectives, police, tabloids
CNN wannabes
you really don't have far to go
look to the man in the mirror
that's who threw the last blow.

Michael couldn't take that upper cut
or deal with that left jab
this beating knocked him off his feet
and kept Michael Jackson sad.

Do you have to be a rocket scientist
or a child therapist to know
that there will be long term **effects**
if someone snatches off your baby shoes
and demands that you now take giant **steps.**

From the crib to the stage
was where he had to go
no time for baby crying
because the baby was the show
(According to Joe).

No bib
no bottle
no teething ring
just stop your inner crying
and get out there and sing.

For awhile I despised his father
but I had to get a grip
I had to process and then understand
that this individual was sick
he only did what he thought was right
to bad his illness became Michaels plight
Damn Michael I miss your light.

You see . . . . .
I grew up with Michael
my plan was to marry him.
sure I was ten he was eight but it didn't matter then
I danced to his beat for 40 years
because Michael became my friend
to be honest with you for awhile in my life
it was just me him and <u>BEN</u>
but now so unexpectedly it all has to end.

But no, I won't stop dancing
and no, I won't forget his beat
I won't forget that its <u>human nature</u>
not to except defeat
Last week I purchased his greatest hits CD
and like that ten year old girl who thought she was going to marry Michael
I ran back to my car with my heart skipping beats.
I tore off the wrapper and put it in
And like magic my car was instantly transformed into a brilliant stage
Dazzling Lights
cameras
action

And I
Sister Deborah Elmore
danced,
moon walked
cried and sang with Michael Jackson
my long time friend
I love you Michael forever.

Dancing with the stars

# MEETING OF THE MOMS

Another child was murdered
gunned down in the 'hood
by someone who has no respect for life
someone who was up to no good.

Someone who simply does not understand
that toting a gun does not make you a man
That he has taken a life that can never be replaced
That he permanently removed someone;
who was loved by many
out of the human race.

What gave him the audacity
who gave him the right?
To decide to pull the plug
on someone else's life.

Tell me
what can we a as a community say to his mother
the one who gave him birth
that were sorry
That we understand and that we feel her hurt
Should we hug and tell her not to cry
While we ourselves are crying deep down on the inside
secretly and openly thanking God that our sons and daughters are
still yet alive
for not one of us knows when the next will die
our children being our common bond
being our collective tie.

And what about the other mom?
Do we hang her by a rope
or do we open up our arms.
And for her too offer hope.

Try putting yourself in her shoes
she was at work
and she thought he was at school
She cannot be held responsible for
a gun he chose to use.

This truly is a game of Russian roulette.
It's like sheep being led to the slaughter
without so much as a guess.

There is no magic button
to make this all end
so we must ban together
and ask GOD
to right now send.

Send out his angels of mercy
Stretch out his arms of love
Comfort those who are mourning right now!
And give them a holy Ghost hug.

Again where do we start
and what do we do?
It starts right here
with you
you
and you.
We can no longer sit still and expect others to do
what we ourselves were called to do.

Meeting of the Moms

# TO THE BROTHERS

To all my jail brothers
Who are currently serving time.
There are a few things that I would like to communicate to you
by simply expressing my mind.

Do you know that each of you were born to be kings
to be the head of the household
and represent Godly things
Did you know that?
Yes, my brother it's a GOD given fact.

Do you know that you are never ever alone
And that GOD is watching over you
everyday and night from his thrown?

Listen closely,
you must understand that no matter what you have done
you can be forgiven by God
through his one and only son.

Don't allow anyone to tell you
That you are nothing
or try to label you a bum
You've got a wealthy inheritance coming your way
because you too are God's son.

When you cry out in your cell
late in the wee hours of the night
Do you know that God catches your every tear
and that for you he is willing to fight

Oh, it may seem long
but brother hold on
because when you are weak.
Remember that GOD is strong.

Do you know that God is a way maker
And yes!
He will make a way out of no way at all
All you have to do is trust in him
All you have to do is call.


God loves you because you are special
Your one of his very own
marked by his love and mercy
soon to sit at the right hand
of his glorious magnificent throne.

So don't throw in the towel yet my brother
Faint not
In the name of JESUS
Hold on.

# BURIED ALIVE

I don't recall digging this big dark hole
but somehow I have fallen in.
Life issues
The economy
Bill collectors
Mortgage payments
A broken heart
Are all burring me alive.
I can't dig myself out
without rocks and dirt constantly hitting me in the eye.
For me, it seems to be raining rocks and boulders everyday outside.

I tried turning to the left
that didn't work
I tried turning to the right
that got me hurt.
I tried kicking my feet.
Maybe I should not have done that
because here comes another shovel filled with defeat.

If some kind person doesn't grab a shovel
and help get this dirt off of me
I know I'm going to suffocate, dehydrate
because already I can hardly breathe.

I don't want to be buried
I've got good reasons to live
I have family
I have kids
I have a gift for the world
It something like diamonds
something like pearls.

But I'll never get an opportunity
to share my gift
if the dirt doesn't stop
and the rain doesn't lift.

There's no good reason for me to cry
no reason to daily feel insane
All I'm asking is for a little help
and I ask it
in Jesus name.
The scripture reads: *You have not; because you ask not* (I'm asking).

# DEATH IS KNOCKING

Knock Knock!!
Who is it?
It's death and I'm already in
Don't bother to get dressed
or to put on you diamonds and pearls
all of that is useless when you travel to the next world.

Look at all your gold and money
and all of the expensive goods.
Too bad you were greedy and didn't share any of it
with the people who are stuck living in the hood
people who were hungry
who just couldn't make their way
widows and the unemployed
living day to day.

All you did was
turn your nose up to them and look the other way
I must say that I am quite proud of you
treating Gods people this way.

Anyways, this is how it is going to go
I'm gonna' take you out of here
and absolutely no one will know.

That's right, I come like a thief in the night
First I take your heartbeat
your breath
and then I take your sight.
Bottom line is I'm here to collect your life.
I've been roaming the earth for centuries
devouring everything in sight
It just does my stony heart good
when people don't choose to live right.

Plus I know you had big plans tonight
partying, drugs drinking fornicating
yes I set the world up nice
with all kinds of temptations so that I could entice.

Thanks to me and my demons
you didn't listen to Gods servants
and get in that silly prayer line
praying, clapping and crying all the time.
I'm so happy because now your soul is mine.

Instead you chose to watch beautiful strippers ride up
and down on the strip pole.
Guess what that was me dressed in all my incognito
you were so intoxicated to high to think
you didn't even see me when I laced your drink.

Why are you looking at me as if
you didn't get paid.
You sold drugs for me
and I made sure you got laid
by the prettiest girl in town (I must say)
I just forgot to mention that she has AIDS.

Then there was that time
you and your buddies found
that case of wine again I forgot to mention
that it was for the church celebration at communion time.

And what about all . . . . the little kids
you could have taken the time to show them the way
but you opted to be selfish
and go back into your hay day
For God sake man your either bald or your grey
that was your hint besides your big belly
that its the teens turn to play.

Nevertheless don't blame me
because the kids have gone astray
It s like the blind leading the blind
so into the ditch you all go.
What can I say
more and more souls.

Anyways, are you ready
because I have to go?
There are seven more men just like you
who choose not to listen to their loved ones
go to church
or go to school
Yes!! that's what I'm talking about
people like this I can use.

Oh yeah
I forgot to say BOOOOOOOOOOO!!!

# IF THEY ARE HUNGRY FEED THEM

If they are hungry feed them
is all you need to know.
don't concern yourself with the circumstances
because these are my children
and I already know.

I know who is doing what
and exactly when
robbing-cheating-and stealing-committing all kinds of sins
you see I'll deal with all of that; when they finally do come on in.

**if they are hungry feed them.**

you see my children are broken in spirit
unable to see the light.
they took a turn down the wrong road
and have lost their spiritual sight
all you need to remember
is that two wrongs don't make a right.

so **if they are hungry feed them!**

and no I am not pleased
with all the wrong I see
so count your own lucky stars
that some of you are not dealing with me
remember that I see in the dark
and that I never sleep.

**if they are hungry feed them.**

My children
that you see begging on the side of the road
digging through trash cans
selling their souls
sleeping on cardboard in the dead of winters cold
look out for them
and in turn I will bless your soul.

I'm not asking you to enable
to be a door mat
nor look the other way
I simply ask you to stand in the gap
and if nothing else pray.
pray for those
who are lost and have simply gone astray.

remember if not for the grace of God
this could be you or yours some day
for the same spoon upon which you measure a man
I will use in the exact same way.

**If They Are Hungry Feed Them.**

# IF THE SHOE FITS

If the shoe fits wear it
and do not get upset with me.
I have nothing to do with the size of your foot
or the color of your shoe
the walk that you walk
the talk that you talk is between God and you.

We all know when the shoe fits
because it goes straight for the throat
then in an instant it has you say:
these people don't know what they are talking about.

Some of you went to the store Pay Less
because of the two for one sale
but the sale is simply not worth it
if it has you act like a tail.

Shoes come in all different colors
and mean all different things
so relax your foot
take off your shoe
and let me tell you what I see.

First of all some of your feet stink
with anger, disappointment and hate,
but I'm willing to withstand the smell
if it will help you get to the gate.

The shinny black shoe with the aligned green sole
is envious and jealous
and on you will do a chokehold.

The pretty blue shoes with the dark blue sole
is cold, miserable, lonely but wants company don't you know

The flashy red shoes
these babies are
dangerous and hot!
They will not come off until they
viciously take what somebody else has got.

The brown shoe
with the beige comfy cushion
is just along for the walk
minds his business
doesn't mumble, complain or waste the time to balk.
You see, he steps light
because he is well aware
that God is listening
and that God keeps all in sight.

He knows when to hold his tongue
that God will fight his battle
and that the battle will be won.

Maybe some of us should consider
simply changing our shoes
the soles are worn out
their pinching our corns
and there staring to become unglued

If not
at least consider polishing
on a brand new attitude.

Again If the shoe fits wear it
and I suggest you wear it well
because those same shoes that you refuse to change
are gonna walk you straight to hell.

# POLITICALLY SPEAKING

Governor,
Thank you for once again allowing me the opportunity to speak.
Legislators, senators, lobbyist most of you already know me as Sister
Deborah,
kind of quiet
kind of meek.

I'm not one to fuss
not one to shout
but I need each of you
to whole heartedly understand
exactly what it is I'm presenting about.

If you are going to pass a bill
pass one that will heal
the city
the community and the state
One that will embrace the nation
and keep everyone healthy and safe.

Lets take a national look at the numbers
and really do something about the mistakes
There are forty eight million people un insured in
these United States.

We have to stop putting band-aids
where serious wound care should be
We have to help move people to the next level
opposed to keeping them on their knees.
Again the numbers speak volumes as to
where our health care should be.

But for a host of reasons there is strong resistance
between finances verses the people's needs.
Each of us has heard the familiar cliché that
United we stand, Divided we fall
With that said let us all take heed and not allow foolishness and greed
to take off and run with the ball.

Capitol Hill
Keep it real
**And pass this bill!!**

# MISSION IMPOSSIBLE

Good morning my addicted friend.
As always I understand that you have been
chasing the white ghost all night
and that you are just getting in.

I promise I will not detain you long
just stopped to see what kind of trouble
I could be of service to you and lend.

Today's mission will be another insane one
except it only if you are in full blown denial
and feel that you can win.

The individual that you will be dealing with today
is some what familiar to you
conniving, manipulative, cunning
baffling through and through.

He has been in our country for quite a number of years
destroying cities
neighborhoods
families
not even the indigent does he spare.

He also has many aliases.

Yes known by different names
but his main aka undercover
is crack, rock, cocaine
not only is he out to destroy
man's body
but to drive each individual insane.

His primary function
is to kill and destroy
with no respect to any person
man woman boy or girl.
the route that he has chosen to travel
is a progressive, chronic and potentially fatal one.

Your mission
should you choose to accept it
is to bring this terminator called addiction down
no more dancing around it
no more acting the clown

As always my addicted friend.
I'll see you first thing in the morning
for your insane missions to start again
this tape will self destruct in 3 seconds.

# MY LORD

Is there one here, who could help me to speak well of my Lord
because he is wonderful you know
he'll not leave you in discord.

Is there just one who could speak of his marvelous works?
For he has been a strong tower to many
who have been at their bottom,
who have been at their worst.

Oh he is awesome and he is mighty
he is called the Majestic one
the king of all kings
the messiah
the one who will always come.

One day when I was out in a battle
I heard my lord call out to me.
he wanted to remind me to put on my shield
so that no fiery darts would penetrate me
my helmet and my sandals
so that I would be covered you see.
Oh I love my lord
for he is just wonderful to me.

So is there one here
one who would help me to speak well of my Lord?
You! Miss with your hand up in the air.
You say that he has always been faithful
that my lord has always been fair
yes . . . . . that is how I know of him
with love and an abundance of care.

So is there one more
just one more man
who could say wondrous things about my Lord?
You sir, I hear say
that he has given to you his sacred weapon
that he has entrusted to you his mighty sword
yes . . . he is the one you speak of
he is the great I am
he is my lord.

Emanuel . . . .
Oh how precious is his name.
is that what I heard that small child say
god who is with us always
never leading his children astray.

Oh, is there one more
just one more
who could help me to speak well of my Lord
you sir way in the back
you say that he is a deliver.

That he bought you out of bondage when the enemy
had you face down
picked you up
cleaned you up
imparted in you his strength
then placed you back on solid ground.
uhn unh uhn.

It is truly my Lord that you all speak so highly of
for where else can we find such a wonderful God
where else can we find such love.

My Lord.

# I'M NOT GOING BACK

Ladies . . . since I have been clean and sober
my ex has been trying to take me back out
he's been trying to convince me that he has never stopped loving me and
that I should have no fears or doubts.

He always whispers that I'm looking good these days
words I've longed to hear for so long
he tells me that he misses me dearly
and that with him is where I truly belong.

To be honest with you
sometimes I get so bothered
that I almost want to scream yes!!!!!!!!
but I know my old lover and how he used to play games
so I know that this is merely a test.

He has been trying to get me to the casino
and possibly to the bar
but this is where my troubles started
because he told me that I could be a star.

He told me just to follow him
that I could go wherever he would go
I had no idea what he meant
I had no idea I could go so low.

You see my boyfriends name was addiction
and the definition fit to a t
he was persistent and he was habitual
and the son of a gun owned me.

Ladies I was so hooked on my boyfriend that
I would do whatever he said
steal, lie and cheat
make money by the things I dread.

But do you know what everyone
he might as well stop calling
because he has seen the last of me.
No more tears no more crying no more stripping my dignity.
Anyways everyone I have a new love
and his name is
Recovery
A.K.A.
**YOUR MAJESTY**

# MY FOUR SONS

God blessed me with four young sons
God's creations, my confirmation
that god is head of my life.

From bottles to bikes
I've watched them grow.

From not sparing the rod
I will surely sow.

My four sons are special
each unique in his own way
my four sons are special.

**I thank God every day.**

# SPARE CHANGE

I'm innocent your honor
I really am.

That's what you said the last time son
when you pulled that ridiculous scam.

But I didn't do it this time
I tell you I was framed.

Then why didn't you just tell the truth son?
why didn't you give your rightful name?

Sir I tell you it's some kind of conspiracy
to keep me coming back
no son, it's the weed the coke and the crack.

That had nothing to do with it your honor
that guy I tapped was just a bum.
What good is he anyways
always panhandling for somebody's spare change.
He begs so much, that's his nickname.

That's the part
that you don't understand
that person is a human being
that person is a man.

More than that
that person is a mother's son.
It doesn't matter who he is
or what walk of life he's from.
You have no right to judge any human being
you had no right to hit and run.

By the way that person died last night
so your charge has definitely changed.
It's ironic now
because maybe you'll be the one in jail
crying out for <u>spare change.</u>

# MONSTER ON A LEASH

Why do you walk around with a monster on a leash?
He's untamed ferocious a man eater to say the least.
I understand that you've had it
Every since it was small
Cute and fuzzy a regular little fur ball.
But your monster has now grown fangs
And the little monster has gotten quite tall.

He'll lick your hand and lick your face
But I tell you he still a monster
Not a part of the human race.
He cannot determine right from wrong.
I believe if you continue to pet and give too many hugs.
The monster will take you for granted.
and get thirsty for blood.

No harm meant but maybe you should consider a cage
Just in case anything happens one of these fine recovery days.

You see . . . . .
My monster hid from me for a very long time
Laid dormant yet played strategic games with my mind.
My monster went to meeting, took commitments
and always testified, about how good God is
and how he now walks by his side.

He was so dressed up in God's heavenly word
I thought the monster part of him had died.
Talk about a wolf in sheep's clothing
I would have sworn this monster was a prize.

This is where tunnel vision steps in and plays tricks on human eyes.
I knew the odds were against this relationship
But I wanted to believe that my monster was my friend.
I wanted to believe that my monster was different, unique
Not a game player, not a liar, and certainly not a sneak.
Even when the little red flags went up
He would say something positive like a slogan or a scripture to cover up.

Then one day out of the blue
My monster wanted to run and play
This was certainly out of character
So I said no monster not today.

My monster always listened and always obeyed
But today he growled and his eyes filled with rage.
He even scratched me when I tried to answer my page
I got so frightened I wished I were somewhere locked safe in a cage.
I tried talking to him to settle him down
But that didn't work.
He started following me around.

Next I tried to stroke his fur.
That always made him happy
That always made him purr
But nothing I tried seemed to deter.

I desperately tried to tighten up the leash
I could now see the transformation from man to beast.
I even tried to throw a few slogans his way
But not even a scripture was working today.
By now my monster had pranced on top of me
I struggled for air but I could not get free.

Of course the monster went straight for my throat
He would not lay off until my dignity, pride
recovery was choked.

You see the monster is really a wild and out of control beast
who will verbally, mentally and physically
rip you apart and on your heartache feast.
He'll tell you that he is sorry
but the damage is already done.
Not only is the monster out of control
But he is a son-of-a-gun.

# HIGH HOPES

No not my baby.
No not my son
He's a good boy
unlike the rest of the neighborhood bums.

When he was a baby
I tell you he was so cute
I can still see him
all dressed up in his little Easter
Bunny suit.

I used to take him to the park
and we used to play ball
I used to stand directly over him
so that none of the other children
would make my baby fall.

Would you like to see some pictures?
I just happen to have one or two on hand.
This is when he was first born.
This is when he turned three.
This is when he got his first bike.
This is when he skinned his little knee.

I still have his first valentine card
the one he made for me
it's a little tattered
because it has been in my wallet
for the past 15 years.

But if you look closely
you can still see
he's really grown into a handsome young man
I've got lots of ideas
I've made many plans
but first he has got to go to college
yes . . . he must finish school.
He knows that in our home
this is the golden rule.

I think he'll be a lawyer
or maybe a great judge
maybe a brain surgeon
what the heck!
all of the above

I could probably go on and on about my son
but I'll just sum it up
my son is number one.

Mom, I know that you love him
but we have another notice from the school.
He has not attended class all week
and he refuses to follow the rules.

The other day
one of the neighbors
said he purposely threw a rock at her glass.
I know how much you love him mom
but your gonna have to take off that mask.

At least remove your glasses
the one with the roses printed on the lens
he's no longer the little boy that you once knew
the one that used to dance and pick flowers for you
because today he is disrespectful and talks back to you.

But still you give him money
you let him borrow your brand new car
you believe every word that comes fourth
from his mouth
no matter how tall and how far.

He's made some bad choices in his life
but that doesn't reflect who you are
it has nothing to do with you being a bad parent
because the love you display
is more than apparent.

God knows you did the best you could
and you've always been a wonderful mom
but he is not a little boy anymore
and you can no longer use your magical wand.

You're gonna have to come out of denial Mom
so that you can deal with this
You're gonna have to hold on to your heart
because I have some news that I must depart.

I hate to break this news Mom
but your son is not a star.
I just seen him being handcuffed
and shoved in the back of a police car

Mom, Mom are you listening to me?
There you go humming that same song
from the time that boy turned three.

(High hopes she got high hopes)

# THE AUDITION

Next!!!

Come on lady
keep the line moving through
you have exactly two minutes
to show us what you can do

What is it that you said you will be doing
what is it that you said you did
a dance, juggle balls, sing a song
what ever the case
just move it along
I'm a busy man
And I don't have all day long!

A poem, poetry
is that what I heard you say
oh boy another starving artist
looking for a hand out today
look little lady
poetry is a good gesture
but this is not a third grade play
were looking for some real talent
so you should probably be on your way.

Hold on a minute Mr.
because I really traveled quite a ways
and the add in the newspaper clearly states
no discrimination
in any way.

All I need is an opportunity
just a few minutes of your time
I am so sick and tiered
of being pushed and shoved
to the back of every line.

You see poetry can be beautiful
if you would listen with your heart
but it's people like you
who won't give people like me
a chance for a brand new start.

Just give me a chance Mr.
because I have been blessed in a special way
if this poem that I read doesn't touch your heart
then I promise I'll be on my way.

Why are you tearing Mr.?
Is it something I happened to say?
You just remind me of when I was your age
and I felt the exact same way.

Nobody wanted to hear the sound of my drum
now look at me today
look at what I have become.

Get up there and read your heart out
because today you are number one
and if you don't mind I'm gonna pull out my sticks
and start you off with the sound of my drum.

Yes I'm gonna give you
The biggest!
The loudest!
The best drum roll
because you little lady have touched my soul.

The Audition

# THE POSITION

No I have not yet finished college
and no I do not have a master's degree
no certificates
no medals
nothing material to honor me.

But I do have something greater
yes much grander than that
I have the masters approval
to be standing right where I'm at.

At this time
in this place
in this moment
there is no mistake.

Understand that it is no coincidence
that I stand before you today
my diploma comes from the school of hard knocks
where God has paved my way.

You see he qualified me to be here
and to do the work I do
to touch your heart
his grace in part
to let you know about a brand new start.

Even if your sinking deep in sin
just call out to God
for with him you can win.

You see he justifies
and validates
that we are all his children
and that it is not too late
for he is the one with all power
for he alone is great!!

You see God is not into positions
or the title or the label that you wear
love his people
help his people
and let them know that you care.

Man can posses all the riches
and have all the prestige in the world
but if you don't have love in your heart
for *Gods* people
your life won't be worth a twirl.

Understand that the lord wants the best
for all of us
every man woman boy and girl.

You see material things will perish
good times will pass away
his word
his love
his righteousness
are the only things that will stay.

We must learn to love each other
and show one another that we care
because the only <u>true position</u>
that *god* is interested in
is of you
on your knees
**in *prayer*.**

God bless

# 911 EMERGENCY HOTLINE!

Emergency hotline can I help you?
Yes my life is in danger can you please send an officer . . .
Hold on please.
Oh my God she did not put me on hold!
What kind of emergency line is this leaving people out in the cold?

Now . . . what can I help you with MS?
Well my boyfriend is after me and this time he says he won't miss!

Calm down now mam can *I please have your first and last name*?
My name is scared to death and this conversation is insane!

Can you please give me the exact nature of this call?
Yes my boyfriend is after me threatening to put my head through the wall.

Well now has he made any physical contact?
Lady he is kicking the door right now and yelling obscenities through the crack!!!!!
Are you able to make out anything that he says?
Yes that he is going to kill me if I don't take him back?

Well Mam there is nothing that we can do about it up to this point.
It's not as if he has a weapon to your head holding you at gun point
It's not as if he has actually put his hands on you.
But if he does give us a call and well send a patrol car through.
CLICK!

911 CAN I HELP YOU

# PERSON IN THE MIRROR

Please don't pass the mirror
because I really don't want to see
that reflection that image
that person being me.

That person is angry
that person is full of pain
that person wears many mask
her own life she will not claim.

Please don't hand me that mirror
because I refuse to except myself
I'm doing just fine
in my own righteous mind
and I will not come down from this shelf.

You see I'm trapped inside this mirror
and I cannot find my way out
I simply don't have enough confidence
enough self assurance
because I live in a world full of doubt.

I would rather say . . . . no not today
I choose to pass the glass
all because I don't have enough courage
to humble myself and ask.

So please don't pass the mirror
because I'm afraid to let the world know
that I am not perfect, simply human
and that I still need time to grow.

# TRUE CONFESSION

Ladies, fellow worshipers
I have a confession to make
I got intimate
real personal
with the lord last night
and well . . . we stayed up pretty late.

Please don't anyone judge me or take this out of context
because my every word is spiritually based.
Anyways the night started out wonderful,
ladies you know how it is when God does a work
He told me how much he loved me
and that he would always be here.
Now this was nothing like man
whispering sweet nothings in your ear.

He knew just how to treat me
and to hold me just right
He asked me never to turn my back on him
and to always, always remain in his sight.

The gentle way the lord embraced me
allowed me to know how much he cared.
He took the time and listened
while he caught my every tear.

He kept reminding me that he made me a woman
with much fruit to bare,
then he spoke directly to my understanding
explaining that he had not placed in me
the spirit of fear.
Every word that he spoke
was like music to my ears.

He gently took my hand
and pointed out the moon and the stars to me.
Right there I felt his awesome powers throughout the galaxy.
With a voice like thunder he had me swept off my feet
the only words that I was now able to utter from my lips
were lord please take me
Enough said and enough done.
I was ready to be set free.

Ladies from that moment on
the lord does abide in me.

Well it's almost morning time
and my true love is still here.
Still making me feel just wonderful
about the night we shared.
Unlike man his word is sincere.

So my true confession to everyone here;
is that I love the lord
and **that I know,**
**that I know,**
**He cares.**

# THERE GO I

I passed a young lady on the street the other night
her clothes were badly wrinkled
and her shoes were too tight
I said to myself
if not for the grace of God
there go I. and I prayed for her.

i saw a man making his way through a garbage can
I remembered those days
I thank God that's no longer who I am.
Yes he was scrounging around for something to eat
a piece of bread a scrap of meat
I felt his anguish his sense of defeat
I gently slipped a 20 dollar bill
in the pocket of his seat
because if not for the grace of god
there go I.

A news flash just came over my television set
there's a woman on the top of a building downtown
screaming that she has nothing left.
Her soul mate has died leaving her behind
she just cannot understand
that it was his season
that it was his appointed time
God please help her to have peace of mind.

As I look around the world
in every face that I see
that person that person that person
anyone of them could be me

If not for the grace of God.

(When I think of the goodness of Jesus)

# I'M PREGNANT

I'm pregnant with my destiny
and I plan to give it birth
I don't know exactly what it will be
but I'm beginning to feel it's worth.

You see God put a dream in me
and in due season
I'll deliver in time
he has placed in me a vision
unique and totally mine
all I need do
is trust in him
keep him close to my heart and mind.

I know that God has not bought me this far
for me to fold and give up now
he loves me
and he cares for me
for I am still his blessed child

He wants me to give birth
to my situation
because I have labored long enough.

No more crying
no more excuses
it's simply time to get tough.

yes!!!!
God wants me to give birth to my situation
be of good courage
and stand tall in the nation.

This is it everybody
I'm going to push on the count of three
1-2-3 oh God!!! here it comes
everyone please pray for me
Doctor what is it?
Brace yourself
you just gave birth to a healthy,
well needed community organization
one that will help women stand up
no mater what their situation
S.W.A.N.A.

# ONE LIFE TO LIVE

One life to live
and I refuse to give it
to someone who is sitting in jail.

One life to live
and this is from the rib
I'm not sending you any more mail.

One life to live
maybe you should have hid
because I'm not scraping up that bail.

One life to live
stop wearing that bib
and running up my telephone bill.

One life to live
I've given all I can give
I'm tired of being stuck
on this hill.

One life to live
And the bottom line is
I'm tired of playing Jack and Jill.

# ADDICTION STOLE MY CHILD

Addiction took my child from me
tore him away from our family
I pleaded with addiction to bring him back
not to harm him
not to hurt him.

But compassion
addiction lacked!

My son was very special to me
he was kind and gentle
very precious
you see.

It's been two years
since my son has been gone
I try not to think about
where things went wrong.
I don't mean to dwell
but this is my song
the pain of a mother
whose son is long gone.

We have no beds!
is what they said
but my son needs help
less I fear he'll be dead

Nothing available!
the waiting list is too long
we don't have the funding
but we are aware of your song.

I'm not trying to blame
or place any fought
but this is a life lesson
we all should be taught

We cannot put a price
On a human beings life
So let's get more funding
And do things right!!

Let's not make this tragedy another mothers plight

# THE PARTY IS OVER

Get off your pity pot
and stop crying all the time
stand up pull up your pants
and force yourself to understand
that you are no longer a child
you are a full grown man.

The party is over
the music stopped playing sometime ago
your just going to have to get over it
so tie your shoes and go.

Go to the next level
the next plateau in your life
if not you'll remain stuck
and you will never see the light.

The rest of us are leaving
we've made the decision to move along
what else can we say to you
change the lyrics to your song
it's starting to get redundant
you've been crying far too long.

At first we felt sorry
for awhile we even felt bad
so we all chipped in to share our precious tools
and all else that we had
it's no easy job trying to encourage someone
who is always angry
who is always mad.

There are those of us
who are starting to believe
that you are not ready
to honor what we have.
it's not that we don't love you
this whole situation is really quite sad

The balloons have all went down
and all the party decorations lay
scattered on the floor
It is up to you to make up your mind
not to live this life anymore.

# THE CHOICES WE MAKE

Who wants to be a drug addict?
NO not one hand do I see
I never wanted to be a drug addict either
But something bad happened to me.

I was strolling along
Minding my own business
Just living a normal life
When suddenly I met a man
Who introduced me to the pipe.

This man was so handsome
I tell you he was cute
He told me everything that I wanted to hear
And on top of that he pulled out much loot.

He convinced me that he loved me
And that I should have no fear
He told me just to trust in him
Because he would always be here
Something about those words
Kept ringing in my ear.

At the time I was going through some changes
And his words were debonair and sweet
Then he lit it up
And I saw the blue flame
This man had me swept off my feet.

Me, my man and the pipe
Was all I was able to see
He kept the room so full of smoke
I forgot all about my children
And how they mean the world to me.

The next thing you know
DCF stepped in
Told me to get it together
Or for my kids it would be the end.

I told them to mind their business
They had no idea what they were talking about
But this woman was hitting everything on the nose
You would think she was living in my house

You see I was deep in denial
and couldn't find my way out
And that man that I fell in love with
Sold my soul to
Had moved on to someone else.

Now I understand what he meant
When he said he would always be here
He didn't mean physically
He meant the burdens I would bare.

Ladies Understand that things happen
Out of the choices that we make
Now If you see this guy within a mile of you
the other road I implore you to take
Don't let him trick you into making my very same mistake
Thinking he was all that
When he wasn't even a slice of cake!

# SHOWING UP FOR LIFE

Who here is honestly ready to show up for life?
I mean seriously
no more drinking
needles, poppin' pills
no more chasing after the pipe
I'm talking about removing the mask
and showing up as your true self
authentic, original
with a heart that can be felt.

I'm talking about that sister
who is ready to stand up in herself
armed with the word of God
and ready to play the hand she's been dealt.

I'm talking about that brother
who truly means enough is enough
no more beating around the bush of denial
no more proclaiming to be tough
he's ready to step to the plate
and be the man God designed him to be
he's ready to start fixin' some stuff.

For many of us
our lives' have been out of whack
only to find out years later
that we've been traveling the wrong track.

Now the question is
what can we do to get our life back
well the word of God says
that God can restore
the years that the locust
and the cankerworm have eaten away.

So not only do we need to walk the talk this time
we need to fall down to our knees
and pray
No more fussing
about who is wrong
or right
Just deem yourself important enough
to start showing up for life!

# SMALL BEGINNINGS

You're like an infant
a baby that can't talk
your just a child
a toddler that hasn't
learned how to walk.
You're not old enough
to eat from the Gerber jar
so . . . . you'll continue with warm milk
until you come to know
who you are.

Through this time
you will fall
scrape your knees and bleed
you'll bump your head
wet the bed
and many times
not be pleased.

For now mom will carry you
at times she'll pick you up
but your gonna have to master
going from that bottle
to a regular cup.

You're going to have to
eat with a fork
no longer just a spoon
no more dribbling
on your bib.
because adolescence
is coming soon.

In time you'll grow
from boy to a man
at this point you'll
have more knowledge
and begin to recognize
God's plan.

Now you're at the head
of the table
and your ready for a meal
but don't ever forget
or despise small beginnings
because they are
what makes life real.

# THE BLAME GAME

We can no longer afford to play the blame game
At this point it does not matter whose fought it is
The next generation is dying
before they get a chance to live.

No point in talking statistics
for many its just too late
were past needing people to step up
We need someone to just grab the plate.

I attended another funeral just the other day
The parents were on the floor
full of dismay
I was so choked up
I couldn't even pray.

GOD HAVE MERCY
We cannot go on living this way!

# ONE STRING

And that's all some of us got
half the time that's all tangled and balled up in a knot
sometimes I sit and cry on my tear ridden cot
about what I have and what I have not
a real pity party just for me
I've invited no one
and no one can see
why do I keep throwing this same party
while still holding on to this one string.

I'm like that woman in the commercial
who has fallen and can't get up
I'm like a butterfly someone has captured
under a paper cup.
Not allowing myself to spread my wings
not allowing myself to step up and sing
Not treating my own self like a human being
Still I hold on to this one string.

Can anyone out there here me
because I'm really screaming out
I realize that its in the form of a whisper
but damn it!
I need some help.

My skies are grey
when they should be blue
some people have nothing
not even a pair of shoes.

I have my string and I should be
grateful for that
I should stop crying
I should stop complaining
I should get up and give my own self a clap
While holding on to this one string.

Strange about this one string
sometimes its a strong as rope
other days its like a piece of silk
offering me no hope
but I've come to understand that
that its all a part of the plan
either I throw in the towel
or I boldly stand.
Still holding on to this one string.

For those of you who have one string
the time has come for you to stand and sing
Right before the curtain comes down
put on a smile and toss that frown
this is your time
and your in the right place
to show the world the beauty behind the face.

If you have one string
don't let it go
embrace it
nourish it
and watch that baby grow.

One string.

# MY ADDICTION

I'm protecting my addiction so that it doesn't get hurt
Isn't that ironic as I stand here without a shirt
You see my addiction already took everything from me
My pride, my home, my dignity
Still you had better step back, step off
because I will guard my addiction at any cost.

I understand that you want my addiction to go away
but imagine me treating my addiction that way
You say that my addiction should be under arrest
how dare you want to put my addiction through all of that stress.

Go ahead shake your head and call my addiction
an out of control mess
but if you come any closer to my addiction
you'll see that this is not a test.

I live with my addiction every day
We go every where together especially astray
when I'm sad, he's sad
when I'm glad, he's glad
people hate my addiction
but my addiction is not so bad.

Many days I don't have anything to wear
my clothes are a mess
and I can't seem to do anything with my hair
Most days I'm hungry with nothing to eat
but its not my addictions fought that I live on the street.

Why can't you just understand that I have a disease?

# A POET'S PERSPECTIVE

From one poet to another
my hat goes off to you
Your awesome
your inspiring
with the diverse dialogs that you use.

It's really quite amazing
the way you mix words up
then lay them out before us
here and at the Public Cup.

You rhyme, you sing
You shoot from the hip
You are truly a unique person
the way you spit your gift.

Some call us starving artist
but our cups are actually filled to the brim
we have the ability to say through poetry
what others can only dream.

Some of us are veterans
some are brand new
but that's the magic
the beauty of it all
being able to share our gift through you.

So again my gifted brother
all of our hats go off to you
For all of your work in the community
making sure that every poet gets a equal shot,
a fair chance to get their work through.

So keep up the good work my friend
that Almighty God has assigned to you
opening up doors and venues
for poets to walk through

We Love you Baub.

# EARTH TO MEN

They say that women are from Venus
and that men are from Mars
But actually were really on the same planet
Looking out of the same galaxy window
but for some reason men cannot see the stars.

They just don't seem to get it
Can't see the meteor storm coming our way
they couldn't see hales comet approaching on a clear revolving day
too busy playing galaxy x box
while our universe spins away
anyways . . . .

Why do they not see that our planet is on a negative tilt
The shooting stars
The big dipper
on this our love was built\
Now every word that comes forth from his mouth
are meteor lies and guilt
I've had enough of this Mork and Mindy relationship
nanu-nanu
my milky way is spilt.

Now you want to bring me candy and roses from
your latest galaxy game boy fantasy
well I would rather go back to school, college attain a super Nova degree;
something that is gonna prove beneficial to my family and me
After that I think I'll spend some time with Orion
because he's always had an eclipse for me.

Orion can see the stars the sun and the moon
He understands that when we look out the window
that it is important to me that he sets his lens on zoom
this way there will be no surprise meteor showers
and our planets won't go boom!
So ladies if any of your men are from that sad planet Mars
There's always Mercury, Saturn Jupiter, Neptune and Pluto
shining amongst the stars.

# BUT GOD

I spent the night with Jesus
he held me in his arms
he told me to stop shivering and crying
because he would keep me warm
he reminded me that he loves me
and that he would calm the storm.

I said <u>but God</u> there's a blizzard
going on inside of me I know that you don't sleep or slumber
but maybe you forgot about me
*He told me daughter just weather the storm
and I will set me free
There are just some things that you must to go through in life
so the world can see you and me.*

<u>But God</u> my heart is broken
and its more than I can bare
*Need I remind you again my child
that I love you and that I care
I know this is this is a tough one
but I gave you my word a long time ago
That I would not leave nor forsake you
and this you must now know.*

But GOD my days are long
and my nights drag through
If I did not have you to call on
I don't know what I would do
sometimes I'm lonely
other times I'm scared
sometime the enemy laughs at me
and yells that no one cares.
*Ignore him*
*my precious daughter*
*he's got his cross to bare.*

# LIFE'S BULLY

Life's bully is after me
and I have been stuck in the house for over a week.
He won't allow me to go outside
comb my hair, do my nails, or even brush my teeth.
Only he can make me feel miserable, worthless, hopeless and weak
because of him
I can't get out
and know one can get in.
Some of you may know of him
his clinical name is depression.

Sometimes he'll grab the telephone
disguise his voice and tell people that I am not home.
You see, he wants me permanently isolated
locked in the twilight zone
while he shoots fiery darts at me
while sitting on his thrown.

He says things like
"Go back in your room
and sit in the dark
Nobody loves you so set yourself apart
don't start your foolish crying
or Ill take away your art."
You see he knows that I love to draw and that drawing is close to my heart.

# HAD A LITTLE TALK WITH JESUS

I got a message from Jesus just the other day
funny how it came to me
it came in a most peculiar way
I had been crying, staring at the ceiling for hours
before I noticed gold dust glittering in thin air circling my bible page.

He went into the book of Mathew
and how Peter walked on water until he got afraid
First Jesus stopped the wind
then he commanded the waves
That's the kind of God we serve to stretch out his hand and save.

Just be obedient my daughter
with the work I have assigned to you
People will come
and people will go
But I will see you through.

He told me that I hang on to things and people
that I should long let go
but not to worry
not to stress
because he runs the entire show.

I have put people in your life
for a reason, a season or for a lifetime
to play an important part
to bring the vision full circle
so that others can recognize my art
don't trip
I always give gifts to ordinary people
because they have extraordinary hearts

Remember You come from royal stock
Your father is a king
He is the owner of a thousand cattle on a hill
the owner of everything.

Understand that the world needs papers, certificates and degrees
what the world doesn't know is that
all anyone really needs is me
my stamp of approval to flourish and succeed
so don't allow the world to kick or knock you down
address you in any manner
and turn your smile upside down.

**Stand on my rock and stay on holy ground**

# A FRIEND TILL THE END

We walked together
we talked together
we spent all of our time together
when he laughed I laughed``
when I cried he cried
our friend ship was so deep
so real
nothing
no one could break the tie
if we only had one piece of bread
we split it in half
and that was all that was said.

Like most couples money was our usual struggle
it lead to arguments and then rebuttals
so we engraved it in each others hearts.
If either one of us make it
for the both of us
it would be a brand new start.

As the years went by we went our separate ways
due to his drug lifestyle I just couldn't stay
someone had to grow up and walk the heck away
but still like a sword in the stone
my undying friendship for my friend stayed.

Hungry, cold, or in need of a place to stay
my friend was welcome come night or day
I didn't care what anybody said
we were friends for life or
until one of us was dead.

I carried with me an undying debt
because he was there for me
when my life was a mess
so for my friend.
My buddy I could do no less
then something happened
and we were both put to the test
my friend
my buddy
the Lord did bless

The word tells us that the love of money
is the root of all evil
and like Satan it reared its ugly head
to steal my joy and knock me down
it turned my best friend
my buddy into the town clown.

His head got so big
that he could not reach into his clown pockets
and give me his friend a red cent
to him I became the enemy
and everyone else was his friend
The world laughed at this circus show
my heart was broken and I felt so low.
I wanted to cry but my mind said no
It won't be long before he eats crow.

# THE GOOD OLD DAYS

Those were the days
dancing, drinking, partying
and plenty of purple haze.
We used to go this particular bar right after work
top shelf drinks were only half price
we thought to our self great! This owner is really nice.

Then came the music
we would dance until the break of dawn
over and over and over
the DJ would play our favorite songs.

Guys meeting girls
girls meeting guys
six packs, muscles
flat tummies and dresses above our thighs
what more could we ask for
everybody was looking good
and everybody was high

Thirty years later
and some of us are still partying after work
We cant see that our bodies have changed
our bellies are protruding and we can no longer tuck in our shirts.

Our jet black hair is now silver and grey
Still we long for the memories of our own hay day
Some of you refuse to move over and give the teens the floor
for some unjustified reason
you want to dance some more

Remember when your inebriated uncle would come to your house
start dancing with your friends
and your heart would scream ouch!!!!!!!!!!!
you would practically have to beg him to sit down on the couch

Some call it midlife crisis
Men with young girls actually believing its him she wants
and not another string of pearls.

Women, beauty comes and beauty fades
Lets all bow out gracefully
And just remember the good old days.

# I GOT ROBBED

911
How can we be of service to you?

Yes can someone please help me
I've been robbed
She knocked me down when I was not looking
and forbid me to call on God.

OK Mam can you calm down and give me your name?
My name!
My name is Ms Sick and Tired of all the freakin pain
Just sick and tired of spending all of my days crying down on Memory
Lane

Anyways Mam can you tell me exactly what the perpetrator stole?
I sure can she stole my passion for life,
my happiness.
This perpetrator stole my soul!

Well Mam do you know the perpetrator
Can we get a description of this thief
She's brown-skinned
She is approximately five feet two inches
brown eyes and a messed up doo.
Well, Mam that's a pretty accurate description of this thief
Do you know this person
Did you two ever have a beef.

All the time
Im looking at the woman in the mirror right now
in total disbelief.

# LOOKING FOR AN ANGEL

I'm searching for an angel at Christmas time
One of God's faithful servants
to help me get my life back on line.
Unemployment visited and threw me for a loop
Now I'm jobless and homeless
and living off of noodle soup.

I'm searching for one of Gods Angels
to open up a door
So that I cans stop living from pillow to post
and off of family floors.

My bills are high
and my funds are low
My credit is shot and I have nowhere to go.
All I ask is if you are truly one of God Angels
Please allow your wings to show.

# OFFICER

I don't want anyone touching, feeling or putting their hand between my legs.
Today I understand that I am my own person
and not anyone's toy or sex slave.
When I say "no", I mean "no".
When I say, "go", I mean hit the road.

Even though I said "Yes" to you 26 years ago today.
You Mr. have been my life's biggest challenge.
You turned my whole life gray.

You see, I don't love you.
I don't even believe I like you,
you and your negative ways.
You have been the slayer of all my dreams.
My zest for life
You've thrown away.

I have been stuffing my feelings for over 20 years
afraid that no one would understand
or care about my tears.
After all, you are an officer in uniform
by many you are revered.

Anyways, I did it for my family.
I did it for my kids.
I did it for your family and friends
because this is how I thought a family should live.

I would say this and you would say that.
Too bad no one else could hear the slaps.
You were an Officer of the law
so you made sure of that.

Anyways big man
I will not be calling you officer tonight.
So you can put away your gun and badge
and turn out the doggone light.

You see tonight I am willing to fight
and to finally have my rights
Lucifer.

# STARK NAKED

Down on my knees
In front of God
I didn't fix my hair
I didn't bother to paint my nails.
I just came to him as I was
because I knew
that he knew
that I had already failed.

I failed the test that he had laid before me
To be kind to all people in spite of their needs
I've been so busy complaining about my own selfish needs
That it took Almighty God to remind me of people far worst off than me.

People who don't have a roof over their heads
People who are grieving for family members dead
People who have no food to feed themselves or kids
People drinking dirty water not fit for a pig
People who are sick with no relief in sight
People who are in bondage every day and every night.
People who have no one to help them along the way
People who won't humble themselves or take the time to pray.

In my nakedness I asked God to please, please . . . . forgive me
I was blinded by self-righteousness and was not able to see.
God told me to go and sin no more
to pick up my cross and get up off of the floor
to be my brothers keeper
and not turn away when people are hurting and suffering this way.

He reminded me that he is the creator of us all
the big, the little, the short, the tall.
That he commands the wind and calms the sea
feeds the sparrows
Now how much more would he do for me?

# UNDER THE SKY

I spent the night under the sky
the waves, the sand, the stars by my side.
Never in my entire life have I been so mesmerized
by the moon, the Big Dipper and how they illuminated the midnight sky.

The best things in life really are free
so no man or woman can take this time from me.
I am living in the exact moment that I am supposed to be.
I am one with the creator; the one who created me.
I felt as if God himself had put me to bed.
Gently caressed my heart and kissed me on the forehead.
He told me to lay back and enjoy the rest of the night
because he had the whole world covered and in his sight.

Around your children and family members I have placed a special hedge
so lay back and relax . . .
Tonight the beach is your bed.

The dark blue sky sprinkled with stars; on it is your blanket.
I've left a cluster of seashells to pillow your head.
I have never felt so alive in a moment.
Somehow I almost felt dead.
You would have had to be there; to understand what I just said.

No cell phone
no text messaging
he said just you and me.
I've commanded the winds
and I've silenced the sea.

The hills and the mountains are your witness that you have spent
the entire night with me.
In the morning I'll send two doves to wake you up.
The sunrise and the morning dew
to remind you that I am still here.
And that I will never cease loving you.
Now rest my daughter because rest you are due.
You have weathered many storms
and I'll continue to see you through.

# WHAT IF?

What if I told you that I lost my job
of over twenty years?
Laid off, barely compensated
and for the first time in a long time
I feel scared.

What if I told you that I was hungry?
I had not eaten in two days.
Would you direct me to the nearest soup kitchen
for a piece of bread and cold scrambled eggs?

What if I told you that the repo man came
and took possession of my car?
Would your heart be inclined to remind me of public transportation
because the nearest bus stop was not far?

What if I told you that I have holes in my shoes?
Still I wear them all the time.
Would you look at me and say to yourself,
*that's your problem*
*not mine.*

What if I told you that life is too much?
I can't take it anymore.
Would you pat me on my back
tell me that you understand
and walk me to the door?

Well, what if I told you that the red flag you see
flying over my head is really blue?
Would that make it easier, more comfortable for you
to be the type of human being who will not lend a helping hand
but instead direct me to a phone booth
and expect me to come out as Superman?

What if you're the person that God is talking about
when he says: *Do not put your trust or faith in man.*

When all else fails, trust only in me and I will help you stand.

WHAT IF!

# IN A WHILE

Has anyone here felt like giving up
just throwing in the towel?
Washing your hands of all your troubles
your many tests and trials.

Anybody here at their wits end
had enough, can't take it anymore?
Seems like every time you take two steps
life kicks you back to the floor.

Anybody here feel like punching someone out?
But instead you stuff your anger, your pain, your doubt.
Now you're the one brokenhearted and walking around with a pout.

Anybody just feel like nobody cares
and that nobody understands
what you are trying to do
what you are trying to say
or your God-given plan?

I just want to say, don't give up.
Don't give in and do not throw in the towel.
If you run your race
stand your ground
you will be all right in awhile.

# BOOTLICKERS

They just make me sick.
They turn my stomach and make me want to spit.
These are individuals who will turn on their own people
just to get an extra lick.

It's pathetic, sad and absurd
what people will do for that one chance to stand up on top of the table
and let their voice be heard.

Sellouts!! For money that will not last
soon to be cut down like a withered blade of grass.
Maybe then they will be tired of honoring and kissing the enemy's ass.

They go in the front door and sneak out the back
deceiving broken people who trust in them while they really turn their backs.
Social status is what matters the most,
forgetting that God is the master of the universe and the number one host.
Living in beautiful homes
driving the best of cars
dressed in the finest of clothes adorned in diamonds and gold.

All these luxuries because they punked out, bowed down and sold their souls.
Every piece of their life appears to be intact
too bad that they have not yet accepted that they too are still black.
Not that it's a bad thing, it's just that with bootlickers like these
Martin Luther King freedom can never ring.

We are one of the most hated,
looked down upon people, despised in many eyes,
but even that is not enough to keep us out,
hold us down
or keep us back
because . . .
Still We Rise.

From the outhouse to the White House to many I say, Surprise!!!!!!
So a message to all the bootlickers
To put your tongues back in your mouths.
God is the seer of all things and you too will one day say ouch!!!!!

# SHAKAZULU WHERE ARE YOU

Shakazulu!
Shakazulu!
All of the women in the village are calling you.
We need you to come back and raise your sons
put the spear back in their hands
but take away the guns.
Teach them the way of the bush
to love and hunt
and be strong fathers one day.

For generations and generations
our jobs were to raise the girls,
teach them to cook, braid
and hold onto their precious pearls.

But our warrior men are out of place
and the young warrior sons are running rampant
all over the place.
They're getting into trouble at an alarming rate
Shakazulu men!
You must get back at your rightful place
so that the family name bears no more disgrace
while being laughed at by the other race.

Even other tribes are laughing
because they know that our warriors
have let us down
basically threw dirt in our face
and left us crying on the ground.
Many of the mothers gather at the village meeting
to try and turn the situation around.
But we are not equipped with the third gift
so our hands and feet are bound.
Some of us are goanna have to open our doors
and rescue someone else's son
hug them, love them,
but take away their guns.

Again Shaka Zulu men
you are totally out of place.
If you listen you can hear our ancestors cry
and turning in their graves.
Sad, this is what they get after being slaves
still they understand the meaning of raise.
Warriors stand up and raise your kids
not to die but to live.

Shaka Zulu, the women in the village are calling you
Shaka Zulu, the women in the village are calling you.

# THE WAR OUTSIDE

Not the one overseas or across the Atlantic blue
I'm talking about the one outside my window
with people who look like you.
War is war
no matter where it's at.
There are guns, ammunition and casualties
people who are never coming back.

Could you imagine gunshots in your neighborhood every day
while you're on your way to work or to the grocery store
and your children are out to play?
Could you imagine telling your child,
DUCK!!! Honey, just go around the other way.

If our kids could only have a taste of life
like we did back in the good old days.
Let's go back . . . . .
back to when we were able to leave the screen door latched but
the door wide open to see.
That's when grandma was straightening your baby sister's hair doubled
over her knee.
When jump rope and double dutch was our biggest battle in the streets.
Remember kickball, dodge ball, and Ms. Mary Mack
hopscotch, pick up sticks and jumping jacks.
Life just seemed so simple then.
Everybody knew everybody
and everybody was friends.

But . . . no something happened, drugs came on the scene
Not that drugs weren't already here
But todays drugs are more prevalent more accessible
Today's drugs are mean!
It's as if somebody sat in their basement and decided money meant the world to them
(this concoction spread like wild fire)
Next, they made an Executive/crack/meth/coked up decision to pull the neighborhood
kids in.
Started holding conversations with them as if they were grown.
Manipulating them by offering them material things that their parents could never afford from home.
Not informing them of the consequences or what trouble laid up ahead.
Not bothering to mentioning to them that if they travel down this road they could
possibly end up DEAD!!
Every now and then I like to travel down memory lane
It soothes my soul and embraces my pain.
It reminds me that there was a time when life was sane
A time when children were not attached to jail numbers, colors and gangs.
Not attached to a mothers heart broken pain.

"The war outside"
It wants our children dead or alive.

# A LETTER TO OUR ANCESTORS

Good afternoon everyone. My name is Deborah Elmore.
I am the Great, Great, Great, Great, Great, Great, Great,
Great, Great, Great, Great, Great, Great granddaughter of Eve.
The first woman who lived in Africa, the very first woman to conceive.

I'm talking over 200,000 years ago. Her genes still resides in me.
So I am the blood of your blood, the flesh of your flesh, no bigger, no better, but certainly no less.

I'm just going to get straight to the letter so that our ancestors can turn back over in their graves and get some well-deserved rest.
(blow the dust off the letter.)

I'm sorry about all the dust, but this letter has traveled a mighty long way to reach our hearts and minds to tell us of a better way. All of our ancestors are quite disturbed. If you lend me your ear you can hear their bones rattling while spelling our specific words. Words like family, culture and community pride, neighbors looking out for one another making sure that we all rise.

This letter is addressed simply to all my kin, there are so many of you out there that I hardly know where to begin. The first thing that I am inclined to address is that my people, your people, all of our families are in deep trouble. Our communities, our villages are in a monumental mess.

So many lives have already been snuffed out, sacrificed, unjustly accused. Our hope is that each of you can see a better day. It truly grieves our souls to know that our people are hurting one another and foolishly acting out this way. From our calculations and from where we lay 90% of our children for whatever reason have gone astray. We have not sent this letter to point or place any fault, merely to open your eyes to the truth that through grace our freedom has been bought.

So to the young male warriors in the village, we roar GIRD UP AND YOUR LOINS!! In other words pick up your pants. We understand the purpose for this action, but for every action there is a reaction and if we weren't already dead, this would kill us. Go to school, further your education and become the great warriors you are meant to be.

To the young women in the village, each of you possess the beauty of an African Queen. Do not throw your precious pearls to swine, don't step on your self-esteem. We the women are the sole carriers of the human race. No natural man has ever been born without a woman's womb in place. And for that there is much Honor.

To the Elders it is up to you to pass the torch, not turn your head or walk away when there is trouble on the next porch. You have been given the responsibility of the head, not only for your own, but for the entire village you should proudly sit on your throne.

# SHOWER POWER

I recently slipped in the shower.
What took place in an instant somehow felt like an entire hour.
I can still vividly recall my fears, my screens and my frantic holler.
Please allow me to set the stage.
No bathmat, no shower bar for me to engage.

The word for today ladies and gentlemen is TRAUMATIZED!
I will never forget the look in my own piercing eyes.
The sheer helplessness that I felt take over me as I reach for the shower door to somehow help me. I gripped it but to no avail; my foot slipped from underneath me as if I were on a banana peel.

It was not enough that the water now turned steaming hot.
My head hit the side of the tub with such force I could not stop.
Worse than that I heard my forehead crack, my heart was beating so fast I knew for sure I would have a heart attack.
I remember starting to lose consciousness but I knew if I continued to lay there that I would no longer exist.

To some this may sound like a tall stretched tale
but I am telling you this fall was a trip to hell.
I would like to say at this time (thank you GOD) for allowing my Daughter to hear my frantic yells.

Off to the hospital I did go.
They alluded to domestic violence
but my answer remained NO!
The shower was the culprit that did this to me.
Burnt me with hot water then knocked me off my feet.
It was the shower that abused me and threw the first punch.
A black eye, two contusions and all I wanted was to go to lunch.

The next day was Sunday and I always attend church.
I am the usher at the door. That's where God has me perched.
My assignment there is to greet and smile when others do come in.
To remind the brokenhearted that God loves them
no matter what shape they're in. and, boy, was I in bad shape.

Anyways, my face was swollen, my eye was black,
my shoulder was hurting and so was my back. But I was determined
to tell the story of how my heavenly father intervened in this attack.
How he sent my daughter to rescue me. Turn off the hot water and set me free.
this was simply not a day for vanity. He gently reminded me of people in
far worse shape than me. Like war-torn countries and poverty.

He told me to be grateful to be able to walk, talk and see because for
many people this is truly a luxury.
So never ever take for granted
The hand of God that you don't see.
He is always looking out for you and he is always looking out for me.

So the message I would like to convey and leave with each of you today is . . .
* First, purchase a bathmat
*Second, check on your neighbor, a friend or a loved one.
*And third, and most important, always remember to pray.

God bless each and every one of you and have a Good day!

# WHO IS THAT WOMAN?

Oh, she is just a woman, a mother.
I believe she is some type of servant.
No, she is a housekeeper. I've seen her in uniform.
Whoever she is, what ever she does, she claims to have been reborn.
How can a grown-up be reborn?
It's a spiritual birth, some type of reform.

I got it! I have seen her before
she is the doorkeeper at the local church.
She is the same woman who encourages other women to stand up and
know their worth.

No, no, no you're all wrong. She is a nurse's assistant I've seen
her pushing the elderly you know people who are aged.
Well, it's been said that she is entirely broke.
Not a dime in her pocket, but in God she has a ton of hope.
I understand that she walks by faith and not by sight.
You know what? We should all stop whispering, gossiping.
I'm just going to ask her because this conversation can go on all night.

Excuse me Ms. but who are you????

I am the daughter of the most high King
I am a child of God. Therefore I lack nothing.
My cup runneth over.
I am wealthy beyond all man's recognition.
All praises belong to my heavenly father for this unmerited position.
Soon I will wear a crown of glory that comes to my Father

My inheritance is:
the heavens above
eternal life. My father's love.
I am the first and not the last. I am the future and not the past.
All these riches because I went through the second birth.
Surrender to my Heavenly Father and you too can enjoy such worth.

# THE SAME BOAT

I wrote this piece simply to demonstrate that we are all equal in God's eyesight. There are simply no big I or little u. We need to know that titles and positions are not going to save us. God is the creator of all, so don't let the size of your wallet cause you to become arrogant, high-minded or selfish. I'm going to ask that everyone hold onto the chair in front of you or the hand or shoulder of the person next to you.

The name of this piece is:

**The Same Boat**

My boat is bigger than your boat
but my boat is better than yours.
My boat is shinier than your boat.
(but my boat has got nine floors).

Well, guess what else had nine floors, decks?
The Titanic.

I'm using this simple exercise so that you may better understand exactly who the heck and what the heck is really important in Life.

The Titanic was an Olympic First Class Passenger
Liner.
Owned by a British shipping company called White Star line.
The cost to build this gigantic ship was $7.5 million which today would equal $400 million.
She was 882 feet in length and 175 feet in height.
20 lifeboats, enough to carry 1178 people.
She was gorgeous, beautiful, spectacular and thought to be infallible, unsinkable, so the captain bragged.

Gold, jewelry, diamonds and pearls all went down into a cold, dark world. Keepsakes and family heirlooms now reside at the bottom of the sea cushioned by rocks, shells, quarrels, murky water and green seaweed.

Has anyone here seen the movie Titanic?
Well, just for a minute close your eyes, (everybody) and imagine that everyone in this entire building is on the Titanic. Cruising along, having a great time dancing, singing and sipping only the finest wines.
Love is in the air and BOOM!!! We've just collided with the huge iceberg which gave off
the eeriest, screeching sound. Women and children are running and screaming and the ship, the Titanic, is going down.

The rich, the poor, the republicans, the democrats, the captains, the stowaways, the cabin boys, the deckhands, the sick, the healthy and the super, super wealthy were all on board.
At this time all we have is each other to cling to, and the only one with enough power we can call on for help is the Lord.

Now, some of us have never called upon the Lord simply because we have put our faith and trust in iron safes and green money which have now gone overboard.
But then again why should he even bother to answer some of us when we don't even bother to treat each other right?
Many actually believing that because their boat is bigger or better; worthless are others life's.

It would only be God's grace and mercy to save any one of us tonight. God help us because the ship the Titanic is now halfway down.

By this time the orchestra has assembled on deck to play its last favorite ragtime tunes. Suddenly the lights go out and all the decks are full of gloom.

The Maestro has changed their rhythm and tune.
They are now playing a piece called (nearer my God to thee).
All people are hugging, crying, screaming, praying and for the first time many are down on their knees.

What we must understand through this poem is that when God sends down the rain; it rains on the just and the unjust, the wealthy and the poor. The weak and the strong. The kind soft spoken and the tyrant we are all in the same boat. We see this when tragedy strikes through earthquakes, hurricanes, tornadoes and floods when these types of tragedies happen we're all in the mud.
This is why we have to learn to care for one another, swallow our pride and give each other hugs.

Why does it take something of this magnitude to respect each other's life. It does not matter how the pie is cut, we are all a piece of the first slice.

God commands the water and tells the winds when to blow
he tells the sun went to shine and the moon went to glow.
Why would one think that their boat is better than yours?
When God is the captain of all our destinies
and he's the one holding the oars.

So my boat is not better than your boat
and your boat is certainly not better than mines.
We must learn to get along with one another
Because for each of us,
time does wind.

# HOLY GROUND

I went before the king today, I kneeled on holy ground
way upon the mountain tops with angels all around.
You see, I needed to speak to my Father the
King, about my many hurts and my many letdowns.
Here I was allowed to enter into his presence where all truths could be
found.
This was a time for worship. This was a time for prayer. This was a time
to pour out my heart, a time to incline my ear.

I spoke to the holiest of holies
and then I listened for his words
He told me that I was his precious daughter and that man's judgments
I do not deserve.
He spoke to me about man's tongue and how it serves as a two-edged
sword, how it can rip someone apart leaving that person bitter and
tart, bringing more pain to an already broken heart.

For he said no man is the Father, not one can stand in his place.
For on that day of judgment he would meet them face-to-face.
So my message is;
Always be compassionate and always be kind.
Think on the things that Jesus Christ would do
and you will always have peace of mind.

Holy Ground

# I SWEAR

One of the things my Mother taught her children was not to swear!
So I couldn't imagine cursing around my mom, let alone at her.
Today I am asking each of you to take the cotton out of your ears.
Hopefully this poem will prick your hearts and
give each of you who need it
a brand new start.
The name of this poem is . . .

**I Swear**

I swear if only my Mom were here
I would do everything in my power to let her know that I care.
I would bring her flowers instead of delivering them to her grave.
I would clean her house, prepare her meals, for her I would be an
unconditional maid (I swear).

I would soak her feet and brush her hair
kiss her on the forehead and wipe her every tear.
I would bring her ice water and tie her shoes
and never, ever once forget to say "Mom I love you."
If I could give her the sun, the moon and the stars
I would hand them straight to her but my mom is too far
(I swear).

I miss my Mom dearly, a special woman was she.
I just didn't realize I just couldn't see
the magnitude of this woman in her entirety.
Now that I am grown, everything makes sense, she knew exactly what she
was talking about, she hit the nail on every bench.
I thought she was old-fashioned, totally unhip, but Mom knew more
than I could ever grip.
It took me to have my own kids to realize this.
Tasty morsels of wisdom she was feeding me.
But like many, I just couldn't see the forest from the trees.

I know now that the sparkles in her eyes were for her family
one of those sparkles especially for me.
It's true you never fully realize what you have until it's gone.
I had a unique, precious gem, one-of-a-kind, a rare priceless diamond
called MOM.
(I swear) if only my mom were still here.

Dedicated to my mother, Ethel

# WHOSE CHILD

Whose child was that?
Lying dead in the street!!
Yes, another shooting
down on oh MY GOD STREET.

They say he was shot in the back.
more than six times.
That's the real issue
Now that's the real crime.

Another mother's child run down by the police.
No weapon found
no motive to say the least.

Did anyone get a description?
Yes, the very same one.
Black teen wearing a dark hoodie
who *appeared* to be on the run.

That sounds like my child
yours, yours and yours too.
When will all of these senseless killings stop?
When will we be able
to once again
trust a cop.

What happened to their code of honor
to serve and protect?
What happened to them in their blue suit?
Being the city's finest
representing the city's best.

This is by no means a judgment call
but some of you policemen
truly believe
that you are above the law.

You must not be aware
of
My lawyer
My judge,
the one who sits on high
looking down from up above.

In the meantime
to the many parents
I send out a spiritual hug.

Now rest assured that your child is safe
up in heaven.
With Almighty GOD above.

JESUS LOVES THE LITTLE CHILDREN
ALL GOD'S CHILDREN OF THE WORLD
RED, YELLOW, BLACK OR WHITE
THEY ARE PRECIOUS IN HIS SIGHT.
JESUS LOVES THE LITTLE CHILDREN OF THE WORLD.

# THE FAMILY TRUCE

This is a poem for all families, who after ten, twenty, thirty
or more years are still going through.
Family members who are fighting, arguing, name calling,
demeaning one another and constantly putting each other down.
Not speaking, won't visit and dare not pick up a phone.
I tell you it's a shame before God for each of us who are so full of pride to
ignore one another's moans.

Basically we are robbing family members of the jewels God meant for us to have.
Spiritually speaking peace, love and joy are really diamonds, rubies and gold.
But because we fight amongst each other, the enemy has crept up from behind
and stole these gifts from our souls.

We must allow God to mop up, pick up, clean up all of our heartbroken tears
The ones that have been falling for years and years and years.
God wants to replace the stony heart with the kind that won't rip or tear.

God said to hand over all struggles, mistrust, jealousy, hurt and pain
Because he is closer than your next breath and restoration is his aim.
God wants us to love one another as he has loved us
More than that he wants us to forgive one another for the countless times
that he has forgiven us.
How dare any of us have the audacity to hold a grudge
When in our own time of trouble it was God who pulled us out of the mud.
He wants us to walk away from foolishness and give family members hugs.

If you are guilty of not speaking to a family member for a day or even a year;
bend down, unlock the shackle from your foot, and pick up the phone
and make cheer.
This poem is for anyone who has this cross to bare.
Don't allow the enemy to just keep standing there.

# ALZHEIMER'S SPEAKS!!

Alzheimer's speaks and Alzheimer's sings
Alzheimer's walks and often pushes things
Alzheimer's laughs and Alzheimer's cries
Many days Alzheimer's enjoys starring out at the big blue sky

I met Alzheimer's about unh . . . . ten years ago
I believe his name was dementia back then
I didn't plan to meet him. He just sort of arrived
Crept into my family's life, slowly took us by surprise
I'm telling you he just came by one summer night.
Needless to say,
the dead of winter came and to this day he has never left our sight

At times Alzheimer's is quiet and just likes to sit long hours in his easy chair
But don't take his quiet side for granted because Alzheimer's has the ability to act out like an angry bear.
One time he grabbed a hold of my blouse and gave it quite a tear.
Another time I witnessed him pick up and throw a fifty pound chair.
(Sometimes Alzheimer's can give you quite a scare.)
You can find your watch inside of the refrigerator
Your favorite music cd in the sink, your cell phone in the oven in a matter of a blink.

But then again Alzheimer's has its creative side
Like artistic designs on your kitchen walls
Using what you wish was paint
But look a little closer and you'll see it aint!
I've also seen him do the tedious work of
gathering hundreds and hundreds of tiny lint balls.

I

One time I
observed Alzheimer's create a beautiful white mountain out of Bounty paper towels
Yes . . . . this masterpiece of a mountain took Alzheimer's quite a while.
Another time he took an ordinary bathroom sink and turned into a cascade waterfall.
Some of these feats are so unbelievable that they will leave you in great awe.

But his greatest feat
The greatest feat of all
is his famous disappearing act
This feat has the ability to create an entire community impact
Police Officers, Family members, neighbors, dogs, news reporters, camera men
searching long hours especially for him.

Alzheimer's Speaks!!!!!

# PRIDE AND PREJUDICE

**Pride and Prejudice**

Never in my entire life,
have I seen such disrespect, dishonor and disarray
Never in my entire life have I witnessed (so called)
Good, honest,
hard working people act out in such away

I've seen the President of a bank
The President of a cookie factory
The President of a shoe store
Get more respect
more __honor_____
then the President of these United States
What in the world is wrong with people?
Their behaviors a down right disgrace.

Could you just imagine if we were under the old law?
An eye for an eye.
A tooth for a tooth.
Could you imagine the body parts that many of you would lose?

For God sake he is the President of the United States!
Sworn in for the people!
By the people.
Into a catastrophic situation that he did not make.

Did we not know that it would be a process
to restructure past mistakes?
It's too bad that after all this time
All theses years . . .
Pride and Prejudice are still in the race.


Deborah Elmore

# MAIN LINE

World Wide Operator . . .
Angelica speaking can I help you?

Yes can I please have area code 1-2-3 infinity.
I have been trying to reach the king of kings the master of my destiny
I have been going through hell and high water
and I'm afraid he has forgotten all about me

Hold on Mam while I put you through.
To be honest he has also been trying to get a hold of you too.
(Suddenly . . .) with a voice like thunder God answers my call
He sounded so Majestic, so Valiant I found myself in great awe

He said . . . . Hello my child
what can I do for you?
I sent so many messengers but they were unable to get through.
You would not step out on faith and take the train, the plane or the boat.
These vessels I sent special delivery to offer you great hope.

I know that you have been going through the fire
but understand that you <u>will not</u> get burned.
I know that situations get hot, hard and painful
but there are life lessons that you still must learn.
Trust me.
I never sleep nor slumber for your very life is my concern.

You see I made you special
shaped and molded you with my hands.
Your unique, your wonderfully made,
in you I placed Great plans
Understand there is no other like you,
Not one in all the land,
who has your gifts and talents,
and I alone hold the master plan.

Satan may make things appear to be an out of control mess
but don't worry my child
for you
I HAVE BLESSED.

# WHAT IF

What are you going to do when you die?
Meet with your maker and walk through the pearly gates.
What if God is a Black man, wooly hair, a broad nose
and does not approve of hate.

What if he says I have been watching you every day and night from my
thrown.
How you laugh, snicker and enjoy the agony of other peoples groans.
How you and your buddies held back, knocked down, blocked, locked
up and shut off
so many peoples hopes and dreams
All because you've been prejudice, selfish, high minded and full of greed.

What if he says I am that fly on the wall everywhere that you go
So all of your dirty secrets I already know
How you threw that resume into the trash
then turned to your supervisor and you both had a good laugh

Did you not read my word written long ago
That the last shall be first
And that the first shall be last
That scripture alone will bring all their hopes and dreams to pass.

When will you people get it?
You cannot stop what I have already put in place
Whether you like it or not, there is only one human race.
You cannot bury, hide or tuck away
anything that I have created is here to stay

Remember . . .
I am God and I am God all by my self
Above me there is no other
So play correctly the hand that you have been dealt.

WHAT IF.

# THE OTHER WOMAN

PLOP, PLOP, PLOP

Are the sounds of my tears.
I've been crying and sobbing for over twenty years.

Why Oh . . . . Why won't you listen to me
I've shed enough tears
to refill the Red sea

You keep telling me that you love me
But you won't let her go
Your lover your adulteress
She's the star of our show

Can't you see she's no good for you
She's proven this fact many times
Still you allow her endless essence to saturate your mind.

I've seen the way you look at her
The way you hold her in your hands
The thought of you making love to her
Is more than my heart can stand

You think I don't know
The many times you would sneak out
in the wee hours of the night.
All because you had to have her
your lover . . .
your mistress . . . .
the crack pipe.

# THE BOOGIE MAN

(5 years old)

Every night in my room the boogie man appears
He is watching me
He is scarring me
He is grinning from ear to ear
He tells me that if I don't allow him to look at me
He will kill my Winnie the Pooh bear.
I keep calling for my mommy, but I guess she doesn't hear.

(10 Years old)

The boogie man came into my room again last night.
I hate him!
I despise him!
Because with him I always fight
He is stronger than me and he holds me down
His sweaty hands, he always puts underneath my pink Barbie night gown.

I asked my mom does she ever hear me scream
She turned her head and whispered softly
That it was all just a bad dream.

(15 years old)

And the boogie man no longer comes to my door
The last time he tried to touch me I knocked him cold out on the floor.
I cry a lot and I act out a lot
I just don't want anyone in my spot

(25 years old)

I don't want to go outside or have a man look at me anymore
My anger zooms from zero to ten
In a matter of seconds it soars

(30 years old)

I have a lot of issues today
Because my mom could not here,
Plus the boogie man tore the head off my Winnie the Pooh bear
I still love my mom because today I understand
That she too was afraid of the boogie man.

(50 years later)

And yes, I am in therapy
Because it is the only road back
to moving **forward** for me.

# THIS POEM

This poem is only . . . .
I repeat only for those who are dead serious and totally
understand the magnitude of our situation and the travesty at hand.

The rest of you can go back home
because in these meetings
We will not be discussing Wonderland

Our communities are in a state of emergency
There is a worldwide epidemic
burning like wildfire across the land
its wiping out our sons and daughters
and as of today we still do not have a rock solid plan

This is not a test . . .
This is not a test . . .
Right now we are calling on frontline soldiers
to stand and give their best.
We do apologize that for most of us there's been no official training,
so we're swearing in, deputizing moms, dads, aunts, uncles, alderman,
church, city officials,
ex-offenders anybody who is willing
to stand up and fight, to help us save our children's life's.

I sit with mothers every week
hearts ripped open
as they weep
you have to be made of stone
not to rise up off your seat
We are our brother's keeper
We should weep when they weep.

It's too bad we have not figured it out
not smart enough to come together and simply hold hands
This thing is bigger than one or two or three organizations
This epidemic is as wide as all outside
stretching across the land.

# ON HIS WAY!!!

**Hear Ye! Hear Ye!**
**The King is on his way**
**All of you who know him**
**Honor and Ex halt him**
**Bow now**
**and humbly step this way**

We all knew that he was coming
We've heard about him throughout the years
For generations and generations his Great name has been revered
Your Parents told you
and their parents told them
Our Great, Great Grandparents proclaimed this Fact to all!!

Jesus is coming!
Yes he is on his way
I don't know the exact hour
the miraculous moment
that divine second
But high horns will blow that day
OH . . . . he's coming everybody
The Lord Jesus is on his way
The sky is going to open up and Jesus is coming through
May God have mercy on me and each and every one of you

Listen to me each of you
who have a ear to hear
an eye to see
and a voice to praise
stand up clap now
and give God the Praise!
Don't continue to take your life for granted
For not one of us knows the day.

The Lord Jesus is on his way

# A GENTLE GIANT

HOW MANY MEN DOES IT TAKE
TO BRING A GIANT DOWN
ONE HUNDED
TWO HUNDRED
OR A FEW WHO ARE **MURDER** BOUND

MY HEART GOES OUT TO THE FAMILY
NO MATTER WHAT THE CASE
BECAUSE BEATING ANYONE TO SUCH A DEGREE
IS A GOD FORSAKEN DISCRACE.

THIS MAN WAS NOT AN ANIMAL
BUT A PERSON
A HUMAN BEING
BUT ONCE AGAIN
WITH THE CAMERAS RUNNING
WERE EXPECTED
NOT TO BELIEVE WHAT WE'VE SEEN

BRUTALITY, CRUELTY
AND DOWN RIGHT BEING MEAN

THE CORONER'S REPORT RULED HOMICIDE!!
OR HAS WEBSTER CHANGED
THE DEFINITION IN THE BOOK
EVEN A BLIND MAN WITH DARK SHADES ON
WOULD HAVE NO NEED FOR A SECOND LOOK
AND YES!
WE FULLY UNDERSTAND
THE MENTAL HEALTH ISSUES OF THIS MAN
BUT THE FORCE OF THEIR STICKS IS WHAT TOOK!

NO DAMAGE TO THE INTERNAL ORGANS!!
(COME ON NOW BE FOR REAL)
THEIR WEAPONS MADE FROM AIR CRAFT MATERIAL
HAVE TAKEN ROCKETS OUT OF THIS WORLD

MAY GOD BLESS AND COMFORT THE FAMILY
OF THIS GENTLE GIANT
THIS PEARL.

SISTER DEBORAH ELMORE
A SERVANT OF GOD

# YOU'R ANGEL

EVERYONE TAKE A SEAT
AND PLEASE JUST SETTLE DOWN
WE ARE GOING TO BE ENTERING INTO
THE PRESENCE OF GOD
SOON TO BE STANDING ON HOLY GROUND

IF YOU WOULD TURN AND LOOK CLOSLY MY FRIEND
JUST USE YOUR SPIRITUAL EYE
YOU WILL BE ABLE TO SEE THE BEAUTIFUL ANGELS
THAT GOD HAS POSTED BY YOUR SIDE

EACH ONE WITH A SPECIAL ASSIGNMENT
DESIGNATEDTO WORK ON YOUR BEHALF
SO PLEASE DON'T MOVE FROM THIS HOLY GROUND
YOU MUST HOLD STEADY YOU M UST HOLD FAST

UNDERESTAND THAT GODS ANGELS ARE OBEDIENT
AT DOING AS THE LORD WILL HAVE THEM DO
RIGHT NOW THEY ARE IN PLACE FOR YOU
TO RECEIVE YOUR BLESSING
WHEN THE MASTERS COMES WALKING THROUGH

OH HE IS ON HIS WAY EVERYONE
YOU CAN FEEL HIS HEAVENLY PRESENCE ENTERING IN
DON'T ANYONE LEAVE BEFORE THE MIRICLE HAPPENS
FOR YOU MAY NOT GET THIS CHANCE AGAIN.

# MY MIND

Has anyone here seen my mind?
I swear it just slipped away.
I don't recall the hour, the month or if it rained that particular day.

I remember trying to hold on to it
gripping, clinging, and practically begging it to stay.
I guess it was all in vain because my mind has once again gone astray.

I knew it was trying to leave me!
I started forgetting little things every single day
like where my keys were, my other shoe.
Did I forget to tell someone special today that I love you?
I lost my diamond earrings, my blackberry and my Ipod.
Walking around in circles, to others (I) was apparently odd.
Just the other day I misplaced my bank card.
I remember putting it in a safe place but somehow that safe place turned out to be my back yard.
God what is happening? My behaviors are turning bazaar.
Even my children are beginning to whisper that maybe it's time to take mom for **that** ride in the car.

But do you know what?
I'm a fighter and I won't let it leave without a fight.
So I began to take better care of my mind every day and every night
I exercised it
Vitaminzed it!
I gave it organic teas!
I did meditation, all kinds of inspirations
But still my mind abandoned me.

So many days I just sit in the dark
Reminiscing about when my thoughts were sharp.
Reading, writing, and decision-making for me
was as natural and calming as art.
I wonder if my mind has any idea that it has totally broken my heart.

Some people laugh, judge, gossip and snicker at me
(but they just don't know)
that in a battle of the wits I used to be *astronomical!!*
My mind was like a well-oiled machine, now all I have left are my
half-forgotten dreams.
The worst part, the part that truly makes me feel insane
the part that embarrasses me and puts me to shame.
is when, for the love of God, I can't even remember my own first name.

At this point everyone decided to put a call into the king and inquire.
God why me?
To my surprise God said, "Why not?"
The same people judged, hammered and nailed me to a tree
Then they placed a crown of thorns on my head
would not stop judging until I was dead.
Then he told me not to worry for where he has gone I will go also.
He explained that he has prepared a place for me where no one will laugh
and snicker at me.
Here there will be no more suffering and no more pain
no more dark clouds and no more rain.
For in this place
the Angels will proudly know my first and last name.

# PRETTY IN PINK

Ladies, it took me all of 15 years to finally face the inevitable.
A little more than slightly grey
the bulge in my stomach just refuses to go away
and my breasts are not perky like they were back in the good old day.
More than that I am a middle-aged woman who has never had a mammogram.
I was given several appointments over the years
but every date, every appointment, would overload my mind with fear.

My family and friends tried to encourage me.
My daughter even took me out to a pink ribbon tea.
What I need you to understand, ladies, is my anxiety.
It is simply off the chart when it comes to taking care of me.
Oh . . . I'll take care of a family member
run around doing errands for friends.
But when it comes to taking care of little 'ole me,
you'll find me on the back burner again.

Anyways, ladies, it happened one Monday morning
While I was at the beach spending time with God
and kicking sand through my feet.

I noticed a Mammogram bus in a nearby parking lot
Something whispered 'This is your day."
So I went to my car, drove over, got to the big pink van and stopped.
I boldly walked up thirty-three stairs.
There were really only three
but this is how my anxiety picks on me.
Before I could change my mind or decide to run
a friendly voice opened the door and simply said. WELCOME!
I quickly started babbling, explaining that this was my first time
that my breasts are very tender and that, maybe, I should come back at another time.
She smiled, handed me a clip board and assured me that I would be just fine.

Next, she handed me a pretty pink robe to slip into
talked me through it, before I knew it I really was through.
Today I know that my life is worth it and yours is too.
So ladies take the greatly feared Mammogram and GOD bless you.
**Pretty in Pink**

# SISTER WITH A NEW ATTITUDE

Sister with a new attitude.
Could that person possibly be you?
Have you finally stopped
wrestling with yourself?
Putting your own self down
And allowing other
people to dictate-define and limit you?

Have you yet come to the realization
that you are not alone
that you are just as good at the next person
and worthy to sit on life's throne?

For you I roll out the red carpet
place on your head a golden crown
all you have to do is take that first step
and don't turn back around.
No more sitting on life's back burner.
It is time for you, my sister, to abound.

You are a Sister With A New Attitude.

# SUPER HERO

Faster than a speeding bullet.
More powerful than a locomotive.
Able to leap tall buildings in a single bound.
Most of us fondly remember this fighter for justice
this super hero as Superman.

But today we recognize this individual
this doer of all things
this multitasking
multi-talented person as
The single mom.

You'll see her out on the baseball field
Rooting her sons on.
You'll find her in the grocery store
while drying six loads of laundry.
Right next door
she's been seen fixing dinner
washing dishes
ironing clothes
changing diapers
and helping out with homework
all at one time.

I tell you this person
is phenomenal.
How does she do it?
How does she keep her foot to the grind?
When asked by the Metropolis Daily Time,
she replied,
With the help of God in her heart
And always on her mind.

That's not counting the forty hours
She put in
For this woman of great accomplishment
there appears to be no end.

No, there's no phone booth
to change clothing
no costume to put on.
This individual steps inside of herself
to get the job done.
She really is a super hero.
She is a Supermom.

# THE WAR

Stare back at your addiction
when it stares at you.
Don't allow it to anyway frighten
or intimidate you.

Don't allow it to insist
that you go back out.
That's not what you want
so possess no doubt.

Your addiction is ruthless
and it has no fear.
So pick up your recovery tools
and put on your artillery gear.

You have been trained by the best
to talk the talk.
Now it is time for you to assume the position
and, by God, walk the walk.

AA, NA the traditions and twelve steps.
You're one of our best soldiers
now put to the test.

Yes, you have been called out
to the front line.
No turning back
no changing your mind.

Addiction is strategic
very tactful to say the least.
Not only is addiction a monster
but it's a mean ugly beast.

Remember that addiction
is determined for you to fall
and never get back up.

So, you put on the whole armor of God
and you kick addiction's butt.

# THE DINING ROOM

Elegant with a touch of class
chandelier lighting in concert with shinning brass.
The chef is at your beck and call.
Good food, good servers, excellent desserts
you've got it all!!!

In all the beauty of the dining room
trouble can stir and give way to gloom.
There are those who proclaim that there is simply no room
for the new kid on the block who is trying to bloom.
Walkers and canes travel from table to table
because of many reasons
the newcomer is not able.

To fit in is all the newcomer wants to do.
But the newcomer is sometimes shunned, or blatantly ignored
left to feel like two left shoes.
Could you imagine someone doing this to you?
Take a min. and put on someone else's shoes
while enjoying your meal in the dining room.

In the dining room friendships can grow.
Hearts can smile, even in the mist of test and trials.
Some are lost, troubled and feeling blue
but most would be happy to sit with you.
My message is:
Let us all treat one another right.
While the dining room tables and chairs are still in sight.
There is nothing more important than a precious human life.

God bless
The Dining Room

# THE CARE GIVER

The most humbling job on the planet.
This particular job consist of pushing, pulling, lifting, wiping and diapering.
The caregiver must be able to understand confusion, deal with allusion and sometimes endure persecution.

The caregiver's biggest responsibility is to protect, because when it is your shift, the family expects nothing less.

Who understands the real cost of being a care giver?
Many mornings the care giver is already drained, because the patient has been walking up and down all night.
Won't listen, won't sleep and at you he may bite.
In one night the care giver has been kicked, spit on and called out of her name
Nothing the care giver can do but except the fact, that for many elderly people the brain does change.
Memory loss, hip replacements and knees that give way
Sounds like patient issues but this is also the care givers dismay.
Even still they can't miss work because the care giver has bills to pay.

Doctor appointments, Pharmaceutical runs,
the caregiver is really an essential part of the family recognized by none!
Now many believe that being a care giver is easy, simplistic work.
That the care giver is lazy, lackadaisical and that his or her duties they often shirk.
But the real truth is that many care givers would give their one and only shirt, for the person they have come to know to be happy and feel some worth.

My hat goes off to the adult children who have not strayed and forgot the way
To Honor Thy Mother and Father until their dyeing day.
You see turning old is like a flower, a natural part of life.
Flowers come and flowers go
Just like the rain that helps them grow.

But even when the flower withers and grows old
It is the CARE GIVER who loves, extends patience and fully knows
That a rose . . . . . is still a rose.

This poem is dedicated to all nurses, all aids, all family members, housekeepers and slaves who work so hard to make someones else's life worth living.
A special thanks to those who work with our disabled population.

# I TOO KNOW WHY THE CAGED BIRD SINGS

I too know why the caged bird sings
She sings for freedom above all things
She sings for justice, love, equality and respect
But none of theses things has she gotten yet.

I know why she rears up and spreads her wings
Why she will not give up on her hopes and dreams
It is not her fault that the world system is mean
and that she remains behind bars that are physically unseen.
I too know why the caged bird sings.

Yes her wings are clipped and her feet are still tied
So she uses her songs to soar through the skies
Her songs are unique with a rhythmic tune
causing her dreams of freedom to suppress her gloom
This is her way of reaching the moon
I too know why the caged bird sings.

Many free birds are the color of doves
But not gentle, not kind and certainly not love.
The free bird glides through the air with his wings spread wide
An accuser of the brethren
An oppressor who believes he owns the sky.
Still refusing to hear the caged birds cry.

And this my friend is the reason why
I too know why the caged bird sings, she sings for freedom above all things.

This poem is dedicated to the Honorable
Mrs. Maya Angelou

*At My Fathers Feet Productions*
*Mr Henry Gatison*

Made in the USA
San Bernardino, CA
26 September 2014